INTEGRAL
GROUP

"Experience matters. Experience at the edge matters if you want the edge to become the norm." **- Jason F. McLennan**

INTÉGRAL: Revolutionary Engineering

An Ecotone Publishing Book / 2013

Copyright © 2013 by Molly Miller

Ecotone Publishing – an Imprint of the International Living Future Institute

For more information write:

Ecotone Publishing
721 NW Ninth Avenue, Suite 195
Portland, OR 97209

Author: Molly Miller
Book Design: softfirm
Edited by: Fred McLennan

Library of Congress Control Number: 2013949816
Library of Congress Cataloging-in Publication Data

ISBN 978-0-9826902-6-0

1. Architecture 2. Engineering 3. Technology

First Edition

Printed in Canada on one hundred percent recycled content paper, Processed Chlorine-Free, using vegetable-based ink.

VanDusen Botanical Garden
Visitor Center

INTÉGRAL

Revolutionary Engineering

03 ACCELERATE

04 SUSTAIN

The Exploratorium Museum
Pier 15, San Francisco, CA

INTÉGRAL:
Revolutionary Engineering
Stories from the leading edge of deep green design

Foreword by Jason F. McLennan, Chief Innovation Officer

I have often said that engineers are the unsung heroes of green design; the designers typically get the most attention, but it is the engineers who make much of the building work. To get better at what I did as an architect, I had to learn to think like them and appreciate their special genius. What I learned to appreciate early on was how critical the right engineering team is in order to achieve exemplary building performance. And yet I also came to learn that "traditional engineering" was not set up to produce innovation and game-changing results. The building industry rewarded sufficiency rather than efficiency, and rules of thumb and prior experience guided the majority of solutions. Engineers often applied the same process and technology and thinking year in, year out, and hindered the breakthroughs needed in energy and water performance and thermal comfort. The architecture and engineering disciplines largely practiced in isolation and sometimes in direct conflict.

Thankfully, there were exceptions to this state of affairs, and in the nineties, prior to the rise of LEED and the resurgence of green building, I sought out this "new breed" of engineers – ones who collaborated, measured their buildings to understand true performance and pushed their designers to improve and do better. Kevin Hydes and Peter Rumsey were two of the brightest lights in the industry at the time – competitors who shared a passion for changing the way buildings impacted the natural world and the communities around them. Working with Kevin and Peter and their colleagues at KEEN Engineering and Rumsey Engineers made me a better designer. We learned together and practiced integrated, holistic design – something bandied about commonly now but rare back then. Year after year I watched both of these professionals provide leadership to the industry – through cutting edge projects, board positions at the USGBC, and important research and innovative ideas. Each of these leaders was training a new breed of engineers in a new way of thinking.

Fast forward to 2013 and Kevin Hydes is celebrating the fifth year of his new engineering firm, Intégral Group. He has joined forces with Rumsey Engineers as well as with the former Cobalt Engineering in Canada (Canada's best) IDeAs (led by whiz electrical engineer David Kaneda) and a host of talented professionals around the United States, Canada and the United Kingdom – quite possibly the deepest bench of engineering talent in the world assembled under one philosophy and culture.

Kevin's goal was simple:

"To be the very best at what we do as building engineers and help others meet that same goal. We are staunch stewards of all the progressive movements and standards that can help us reach our vision...I believe in the power of one ....and the power of many."

The engineering firm celebrated in this book has relied on revolutionary strategies and tactics, not just to grow into the influential firm it is today, but also to radically re-chart the course of green design. Intégral and its people have helped change the way all of us – engineers, architects, owners and occupants – will live in and grow with our buildings in the coming decades. I, for one, am excited to see what they do next.

Officially, I serve as Intégral's Chief Innovation Officer as well as continuing to serve the broader movement through my work with the International Living Future Institute. The opportunity to work alongside these pioneers was too interesting to pass up and the potential to move the needle on regenerative design too important to let slip.

Unofficially, I think of myself as more of a beneficiary of the firm's genius. One of the most profound lessons I have had reaffirmed along the way is that engineering – mechanical, electrical, plumbing, lighting – is really the linchpin of green building success. Thinking differently as engineers is key to the transformation we seek in reaching net zero energy and Living Buildings. Intégral engineers have taught me that we will never get where we need to go if we do not fundamentally transform our methodology of engineering, designing and imagining what we build. It is possible to create a living future, but only if we commit to wholly different ways of thinking. Success depends on widespread change, committed to and practiced by every professional in all disciplines.

This book highlights the leadership and ideas of many individuals in the firm, inspiring their colleagues and clients to do what they do every day: imagine, perform, accelerate and sustain, four words that guide the culture and vision in Intégral as explained further inside these pages. It explores numerous examples of how Intégral is changing the field, one project at a time. Yet, ultimately for Intégral to be successful at reaching its goals there is the important realization that it has to do so in the context of a changed profession. It is not enough to make change one building at a time, or to change a single firm when the state of the environment is as periled as it is today.

The new engineers have to take a different approach towards "competition" and learn to share and teach each other. They must pass on the lessons learned to other engineers, architects and building owners. This book is offered in that spirit. Thankfully, there is a growing cadre of deep green engineers in many firms who share this passion and philosophy and we trust that this publication further strengthens their resolve and effectiveness. We hope that this book inspires architects to collaborate more completely and to include building performance as a first priority. We also hope that this book will inspire building owners and developers to reach higher with their projects and to demand excellence from their design teams. In short, we want this book to play an important role in changing the way all of us who shape the built environment think and practice.

Inside are fascinating stories of success and failure and the underlying principles and philosophy that guide Intégral. Returning to Kevin Hydes and his vision:

"This is not a story of an individual or individuals; this is a story about a movement, and a community. It is a story of commitment, passion, desire, belief and, above all else, a commitment to relentless momentum."

Anyone interested in getting involved in this peaceful revolution will learn plenty in the pages of *Intégral: Revolutionary Engineering*. Read on, and join us with relentless momentum as we push our projects and our practices forward.

Imagine, Perform, Accelerate, Sustain

A letter from Kevin Hydes, Founder and CEO Intégral Group

I grew up in post-industrial Britain in the northern city of Leeds, with its belching coal-fired power plants and coal from the local Yorkshire mines burning in every house. As kids, we used to throw stuff in the canal; that's just what you did.

I now live in Berkeley with my wife and two daughters who insist on recycling and composting nearly everything in our house. My office in Oakland is pretty close to zero waste. And as an engineer, I've dedicated nearly the last two decades doing my best every day to cultivate a community of green building professionals, all dedicated to transforming the building industry toward sustainability. Needless to say, I've changed a bit since I left Leeds.

But my interest in green design did not originate from an environmental epiphany as much as the fact that I've had the opportunity to work with amazing people on buildings that allowed me to more authentically embrace my training as an engineer.

Engineers are trained to solve problems. Working on large campus buildings in the 90s, I found I was installing these very big, complex systems for important clients and continually adding on to them. We design systems to heat, cool or ventilate, or whatever the problem is we are trying to solve. Then, when our clients start operating our buildings, we often find we have another problem, say a pump that's not working or a fan blade that is stuck. So we add a widget, called a valve, to fix the first problem and another widget, called a gasket, to fix the second problem.

Before you know it, you have multiple layers of systems with increasing complexity, all to solve often very simple problems. When you create these buildings that are so complex from the beginning that you can barely operate them without continuous training and know-how, before you know it you are really far away from the problem you were originally solving and ironically you, as engineer, have become part of the problem.

There are often conflicting and counterproductive processes at play. As engineers we usually get paid more if the system we put in is bigger. We are paid for sufficiency instead of efficiency and there are built-in disincentives to innovate or take risks. These are systemic flaws in the design and construction industry that are really holding back creativity and innovation and the responsible right sizing or downsizing of needless systems. It takes a brave engineer to seemingly eliminate the basis for his or her work!

Yet I believe that the essence of green building is simplicity and elegance. Green building should rely on users taking more control and being more responsible and connected—not more automated and disconnected. My career has been completely about this transformative reversal since I worked on a pivotal project on the University of British Columbia campus called the C.K. Choi building. The project was designed with the goal of having no active systems and no hard-wired connection to the campus infrastructure.

Begun in 1993 before LEED green building standards was even an idea, the focus on reducing energy, water and resource use was unprecedented. The School of Architecture's Dr. Ray Cole brought the idea of sustainability to the University, and to me personally. This is where I also first met Bob Berkebile who changed my career direction. Ray and Bob gave me the opportunity to really think the way I was trained to think as an engineer for the first time, using the fewest systems in the most efficient way possible and even to eliminate completely technologies that I had built my career on. They are both friends and mentors to this day and C.K. Choi stands as one of the earliest and most important icons of the responsible way to build.

I began Intégral five years ago after spending a decade as one of a number of focused believers who helped lead and build the global green building movement. I had met many amazing people I wanted to work with along the way and realized the demand for green building solutions had outstripped the supply. I set forward from that moment to build Intégral as a global leader in deep green engineering and systems design and delivery. We have come a long way since then and now we are influencing some of the largest and most influential clients and projects in the world.

Intégral Group is focused on sustainability because we believe that net zero energy buildings and Living Buildings need to become the norm within a generation, and we want to help provide the people and the professional capacity to make this happen. We also believe this is good business. It is

VanDusen Botanical
Garden Visitor Center

sustainable for our firm. We want to do this kind of work because it inspires us and we want the industry to embrace it because it both inspires and results in a better product. We see ourselves as agents of change... catalysts. A big part of fulfilling that mission is through sharing information, ideas and inspiration and this book plays an important role in that purpose.

We created *Intégral, Revolutionary Engineering* to tell some of the stories of our deep green designs and the important philosophies and ideas behind this new engineering. We are open about sharing the obstacles and lessons learned, including our failures, to look ahead to where we need to go together as an industry. These stories aren't case studies or a list of facts and strategies. They are stories arranged to illustrate the philosophical pillars our firm is founded and operates on: Imagine, Perform, Accelerate, Sustain.

Every one of our breakthrough projects has taken one individual, one champion, somebody in the firm, who has found the right areas of mutual interest between what we're trying to do and what the client wants to do. Creating trust is a completely non-technical skill yet it has a bigger weight in terms of leadership than technical knowledge, even in an engineering firm. The ability to convince people to try something innovative is something you can only gain through experience combined with passion. Mostly, innovation requires personal leadership and conviction and teamwork. A lot of this book is about that way of thinking and these kinds of champions, many of whom I am proud to work with at Intégral. Some of their stories come from earlier in their career before they joined Intégral, but most of these projects carry on under the Intégral umbrella today.

Some of the buildings we talk about here are famous firsts—the first net zero lab, the largest net zero museum, the first large net zero scale office on a standard budget to name a few. Some are smaller projects where we've learned really important lessons. The designers share a little of the inside story or a more personal perspective on what went on, and sometimes what went wrong, during the design process. They share what they imagined. The buildings all fall into the category of inspiring, worthy of replicating, worthy of scaling up—even those that ended up differently than we imagined. They set new standards. We, as an industry, build on these successes and lessons.

I didn't start off as an environmentalist when I was a youngster kicking around the edges of the canal in Leeds, but today I am. I recently spoke before my daughter's class with some other parents who came to talk about their careers. I went after the fireman, so it was tough. We all listened with fascination as he explained how he goes into burning buildings and saves lives. Kids understand what firemen do to serve humanity, and getting them excited about engineering seemed like a challenge. But these kids have an environmental awareness my generation did not have. And, I'm sure they could tell, I really am proud of engineering. Sustainable design saves lives as well. As the stories in this book show so well, deep green engineering can inspire us, teach us, improve our lives and help us overcome many of our greatest challenges. When the kids asked me, "what do engineers do?" I answered with evolving confidence: Engineers solve problems.

Imagine, Perform, Accelerate, Sustain

IMAGINE is the endless world of opportunity when we think about different ways to reinvent and redefine what is possible in buildings and systems. When we imagine, the infinite becomes possible.

PERFORM is how you get to what you can imagine. Perform is the bridge between Imagine and Sustain. We should be able to confidently predict performance in buildings with today's technologies. But this is just a starting point, not an end unto itself. We have to think about design as a journey. We are headed into an evolution of design based on performance and operation rather than just creating the structure. Innovation is dependent on learning from buildings.

ACCELERATE is really simple. For every building we are building in San Francisco, they are building 10,000 more in China, so we need to do whatever we can quickly to influence how all those other buildings get built, so they are more sustainable, use less energy and pollute less. Accelerate is how we share. We do this by setting examples and through partnering with firms around the world. We also do it through our strategic advisory positions with organizations like the Clinton Foundation and through publishing, presenting and teaching.

SUSTAIN is how we evolve our services. We can build one green building at a time, or we can design our communities to be resilient and sustaining by seeing them as connected to each other, to neighborhoods, to infrastructure and, of course, to the environment. Innovation happens all the way along the line, or the circle, if you add the feedback from performance back into the imaginative part of designing buildings and communities.

IMAGINE

IDeAs Net Zero Office

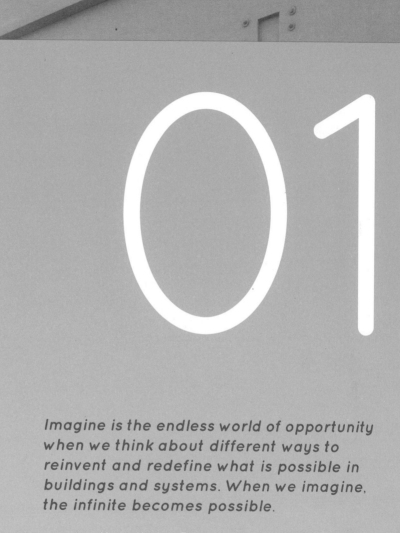

01

Imagine is the endless world of opportunity when we think about different ways to reinvent and redefine what is possible in buildings and systems. When we imagine, the infinite becomes possible.

— Kevin Hydes, Founder and CEO Intégral Group

Imagine

How many chillers will it take to cool the building? That's one kind of engineering question.

Can we spray water on the roof, let it naturally cool down at night and then use it the next day to cool the building? Is there something better than heating and cooling air? Can we heat and cool the surfaces themselves by running hot and cold water along the beams or under the floors? Can we take heat from one place that needs to be cool and move it to another place that needs to be warm? Can we use the constant temperature of the earth? What's around the building? How will the design change the occupants, the visitors, the neighborhood, the building industry, the future?

These are entirely different kinds of engineering questions, asked by a different kind of engineer.

Engineering as a discipline has a foundation of mathematics and science. It requires knowledge of thermodynamics and laws of motion, an ability to apply calculations to determine air and water flow, an understanding of how systems can provide enough heating and cooling and fresh air to make a building operational. This is standard engineering. Sustainable design requires these same foundations yet also requires a kind of profound curiosity and creativity that leads to transforming standard design to be more innovative; more imaginative.

"We need to imagine where we want to go, and that's how we know where to start," says Kevin Hydes, Founder and CEO Intégral Group.

"My personal view of engineering is that on a foundational level you have to know the solution before you do the calculation," Hydes elaborates.

With what we now understand about the environmental crisis, for example, we know we must calculate so our projects will hit net zero energy, waste and water

> "Imagine a world where buildings make people healthier, happier, and more productive, creating delight when entered, serenity when occupied, and regret when departed."
>
> – Amory Lovins

and hit efficiencies as low as 15 kBtu/sf/yr EUI, continuing to perform at those levels or better. As part of high-performance design, we also have the opportunity to look ahead, ask imaginative questions and design our calculations around creative solutions that achieve greater occupant comfort and happiness.

How, for example, can we have lots of daylight and not have glare and excess heat gain in our interiors? If you stop thinking so much like an engineer or architect and start thinking more like an artist, you might find a good answer, according to Associate Principal Geoff McDonell.

"I come from a family of artists and all of them have north facing studios with clerestory windows to capture that diffused light because they realize direct glare sunlight is bad and diffused ambient light is beautiful and comfortable. That's unfortunately what some designers have forgotten," says McDonell.

"Back in the passive design age we had 'punched' windows," he explains. These windows were inset on the warm side of the wall, the insulated side, which cut out the thermal bridging and gave a little bit of shading from the side and overhead. An inset window provides a better quality of light and some efficiency.

In Vancouver, where McDonell works, the glass look is very popular with architects but there's a trend toward using a lot more fritted glass to capture this diffused look the artists love.

This is pretty basic stuff for green design, yet the principle that looking at a building with an artist's eye not only leads to more beauty but better engineering is one that can go much further as we imagine new kinds of buildings.

The Engineer as Artist

The engineer as artist is an interesting idea, according to Jason F. McLennan, founder of the Living Building Challenge and Intégral's Chief Innovation Officer.

"Traditionally, the engineer wanted to practice almost as an invisible profession where the things the engineers are involved with are things you don't see and the only time the engineer got feedback was when something was broken," he says, "and that led to people over sizing systems so they had an adequate sufficiency and they didn't worry about efficiency and innovation. And it also led to complacency and often just a lack of artistry because they didn't think it mattered. Rules of thumb and tried and true practice has dominated the field."

"When you have projects where the engineering becomes part of the architecture, where the duct design has to be beautiful and where the systems are going to be revealed, I think that calls for the best out of the profession. That's what's needed for the new engineer...to not think 'well, it doesn't really matter how I run my pipes or my ducts because no one is really going to see them,' he reflects. "When you say it all matters, you start to innovate."

The David and Lucille Packard Foundation is one of many examples of that kind of artistry. Why is this building beautiful? The architecture is elegant. And the engineering integrates in a perfectly graceful way. The light, the natural ventilation and connection to the outdoors influence the beauty, the feeling, the atmosphere, as much as they change ventilation, lighting, and energy use. The building is net zero, but the systems are about so much more than energy. They are about the health and happiness of the occupants. Beauty, character, emotion are intrinsically part of green design and in a building like this, engineering as a discipline goes from almost invisible to almost sexy.

The "imagine" factor plays a leading role in every green design and constraints cause designers to imagine even more. The Empire State Building, for example, is a historic building with more than 6,500 significant art deco windows that had

David & Lucille
Packard Foundation

"INNOVATION IS NOT THE SAME AS INVENTING SOMETHING NEW. IT BEGINS WITH ASKING QUESTIONS ABOUT THE WHOLE SYSTEM AND PERHAPS ASSEMBLING OLD THINGS IN NEW WAYS. IT BEGINS WITH WHAT BUSINESS TENDS TO CALL VISION. DESIGNERS MIGHT CALL IT CREATIVITY. BUDDHISTS CALL IT AWARENESS."

been reglazed at significant cost relatively recently. At first blush, you might think putting in energy-efficient windows would violate the building's historical integrity or be cost prohibitive. But, imagine taking them all out and filling them with insulating krypton/argon gas and putting them all back in without the glass ever even leaving the building. You preserve the profile of the historic windows yet, at minimum cost, you drastically increase energy efficiency.

"In buildings, when we start out with a blank piece of paper, that gives lots of opportunity for creativity, but a lot of times we're assembling what's been done before," reflects Hydes.

Innovation is not the same as inventing something new. It begins with asking questions about the whole system and perhaps assembling old things in new ways. It begins with what business tends to call vision. Designers might call it creativity. Buddhists call it awareness.

"High performance design engineers see the sun differently and they see buildings differently," explains Peter Rumsey, Intégral's Chief Technology Officer. "When I look at a building I see energy loss and energy waste. We start looking at light and energy and asking if we are using it wisely. When I fly over buildings, I see roofs as places where PV panels should go. Every roof is a potential sea of resources."

The idea that waste is irrational and ugly defines excellent engineering in its purest sense. And then to look at a space and see something that's not there, to look at emptiness and see only potential for transformation, that defines imagination.

Someone had to imagine net zero energy use in large commercial buildings. Someone had to imagine beyond LEED, the then highest standard, and set a new standard. Today, there is a newly established certification process for net zero buildings administered by the International Living Future Institute, and IDeAs, Intégral's San Jose office, was the first in the world to reach it.

The First Certified
Net Zero Office

The concept of net zero as a trend and every net zero building in the United States owes a small debt to the IDeAs building. Formerly the headquarters of Integrated Design Associates Inc. (IDeAs), an electrical engineering, daylighting, and lighting design firm that became part of Intégral Group, the delightful space is now home to Intégral Group's San Jose team.

David Kaneda, owner of IDeAs, bought the building, a 1970s branch bank, in 2005 to retrofit for his team's office. He now enjoys showing visitors the before and after shots, a once dark box transformed into a bright and airy space. "After the Watts riots in LA in the 60s, the bank built their branches with no windows at all," he says walking though an open area now awash in sunlight from sliding glass doors, side windows and skylights. The shape of the building is the same, but there's little resemblance in feel to the old bank, save for the vintage metal and concrete vault the design team left as an architectural feature in what is now a conference room.

To design the retrofit, Kaneda assembled a team of the usual suspects he has often worked with, a team he selected because they are always pushing for greater energy savings and trying new ideas. The team included architect Scott Shell of EHDD Architecture, Peter Rumsey on mechanical engineering, Tipping Mar on structural engineering, and his own electrical engineering team.

"The first day we got everybody at the table and we were having this discussion with the team and I told them, 'I want to make this into a Platinum building,'" Kaneda recalls.

"Shell and Rumsey said, 'What if we make this really energy efficient and put enough PV on to forgo energy use?'"

Kaneda was reluctant. "I was so focused on Platinum; I wanted the plaque," he remembers. In 2005, this was the cutting edge of green architecture, so he didn't feel he could afford both Platinum and zero energy.

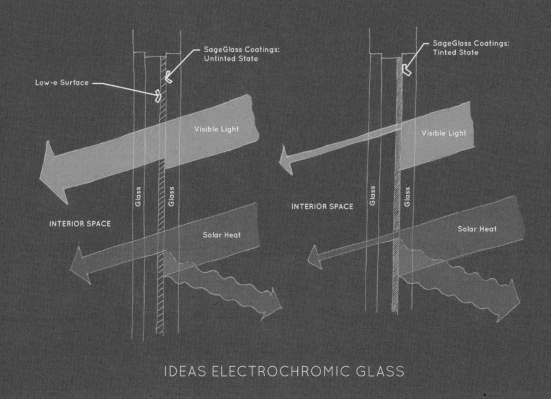

IDEAS ELECTROCHROMIC GLASS

Kaneda went home and told his wife and business partner Stephania his dilemma. "She asked me, 'who are you trying to impress, the public, or experts in designing cutting edge, energy-efficient buildings?'" says Kaneda.

He realized his wife and his team were on the right track. The best way to show off his ability to handle lighting and minimize energy use to his clients was to forgo fossil fuel, and one of the first net zero energy buildings in the United States was born.

To make the building net zero, the team looked at lighting, HVAC, and plugs. The lighting is all about daylighting. Occupants have a view out sliding glass doors and windows. A grid of skylights covers five percent of the roof and provides nice even light levels throughout the day. East facing window glass is electrochromic, meaning the glass controls dynamically changing light transmission and solar heat gain values to limit glare from the direct morning sun, provide optimal light levels, and reduce heat gain. In the afternoon the electrochromic glass reverts to a high transmission, clear state to maximize available daylight. All other windows, sliding glass doors and skylights employ high performance low-e, double pane glass.

IDeAs Net Zero Office

All lighting is high efficiency and the team applied a task ambient lighting strategy to reduce energy use when daylight is not available. Daylight harvesting photocells dim, then turn off light fixtures throughout the day and occupancy sensors turn off lights in unoccupied spaces. A combination of astronomic time clocks and occupancy sensors controls exterior lighting. Efficient HVAC systems include radiant heating and cooling, a ground source heat pump, and dedicated outside air ventilation combined with natural and displacement ventilation.

This project was one of the first in the United States to take a comprehensive look at minimizing plug loads. The design team bought efficient office equipment and innovative automatic controls incorporating occupancy sensors and they set up the security system to switch off plug loads. Many of these features are standard in net zero or low energy buildings today.

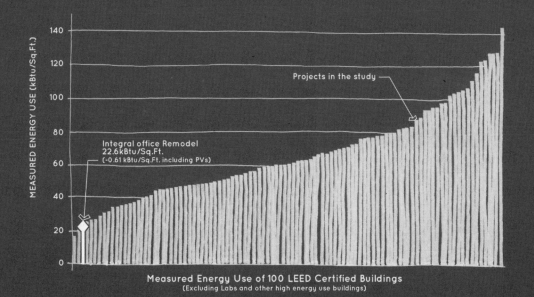

IDEAS – COMPARISON TO LEED PROJECTS

Projects in the study

Integral office Remodel
22.6kBtu/Sq.Ft.
(-0.61 kBtu/Sq.Ft. including PVs)

MEASURED ENERGY USE (kBtu/Sq.Ft.)

Measured Energy Use of 100 LEED Certified Buildings
(Excluding Labs and other high energy use buildings)

SOURCE: New Buildings Institute: "Energy Performance of LEED for New Construction Buildings". March 4, 2008

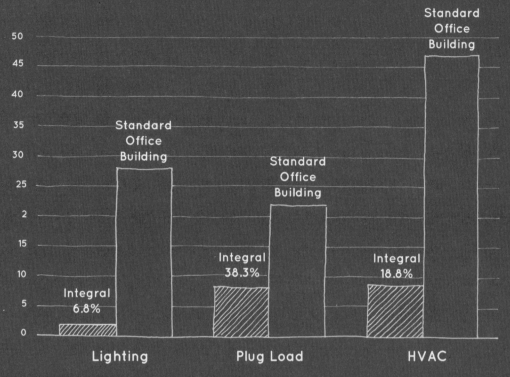

Energy Use kBtu/Sq.ft. - Year

Lighting	Plug Load	HVAC

Standard Office Building

Integral 6.8%

Standard Office Building

Integral 38.3%

Standard Office Building

Integral 18.8%

Standard office data source: EIA 2005

IDEAS ENERGY USE VS STANDARD

The team also installed monitoring equipment to gather data on the energy performance of all building systems. Measuring the performance helps the building owners continue to refine control strategies and test new ideas. The monitoring also allowed the building to become the first net zero building officially certified by the Living Building Challenge in 2012. All certified net zero buildings must prove performance for one year after occupancy. They also must meet standards of beauty and site. As a retrofit of an existing building on a previously developed lot, site issues were not a problem. The design team created

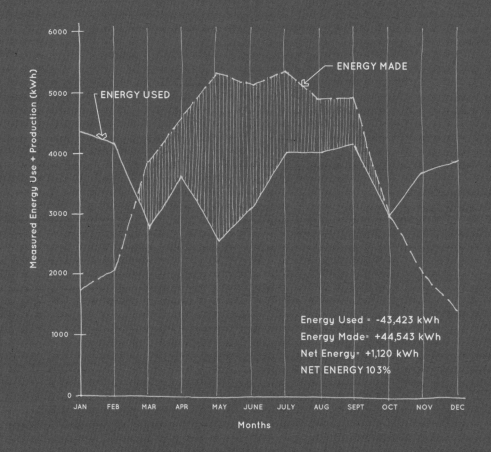

IDEAS – NET ENERGY USAGE

a beautiful interior space for people to work in and Kaneda turned the parking lot into a patio and landscaped outdoor space, providing outdoor meeting areas and views of blooming native plants, which helps with the beauty quotient.

IDeAs continues to improve its performance and is now participating in California's Best Building Challenge, in which participants commit to reduce their building energy, water and waste by 20 percent in two years.

The First Net Zero Laboratory

Though larger and with far greater demands for energy than the IDeAs building, J. Craig Venter Institute's (JCVI) new laboratory incorporates many of the same principles to get to net zero—an efficient envelope, PV, daylighting, operable windows, efficient lighting, and reduced plug loads.

The 45,000-square-foot JCVI lab, under construction on the University of California, San Diego campus, opening in November, 2013, is the first significant lab building in the United States, and possibly the world, that is a net zero energy lab. "It's also beautiful architecture and a beautiful location overlooking the Pacific in La Jolla," says Rumsey, who, along with his team at Intégral, designed the systems for the lab.

The larger imaginative questions that drove the design were: Can we make a hugely energy intensive genomics laboratory operate at net zero? Can we make it resilient to disaster so that it can continue to operate even if there are significant disruptions? Can we also make it comfortable, healthy and inspiring for scientists who are attempting to solve some of the world's greatest scientific challenges? All questions required stretches of the imagination due to constraints and energy demands. While it was possible to imagine answers, not quite all of the solutions the team imagined to make the building more resilient have quite been invented yet.

A great deal of the credit for the forward looking and ambitious nature of this building goes to J. Craig Venter, Ph.D., founder and CEO of JCVI, a scientist most known for sequencing the first draft human genome and constructing the first synthetic bacterial cell. He and his teams have blazed new trails in genomics first by sequencing the genomes of biologically significant organisms, then by creating new fields such as environmental genomics and synthetic genomics. The JCVI is a not-for-profit, genomic research organization with approximately three hundred scientists and staff dedicated to human, microbial, plant, synthetic and environmental genomic research, and the exploration of social and ethical issues in genomics. Part of that work includes a commitment to help solve global issues such as climate change and degradation of the planet's oceans and soils.

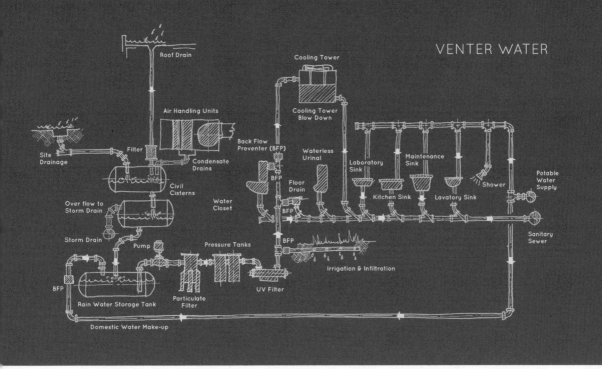

Venter is not just a scientist. "He's one of the smartest scientists in the world and smart enough to want a net zero building," Hydes comments.

Dr. Venter stated his desire that the new laboratory be carbon neutral—and not by buying carbon offsets. Rumsey then championed net zero electricity using PV panels and high efficiency building systems. "We designed the whole building as a huge photovoltaic array," says Rumsey. The entire electrical load for the building is generated from the roof PV panels. Sounds simple, but the roof is small and the energy load is great.

Kaneda, who did the electrical engineering on the building, explains: "We wanted the lab to be net zero, yet we had intense lab requirements like a high number of air changes and hoods and a lot of lab equipment. We were struggling to get enough PV on the roof without compromising the daylighting, which we needed to reduce lighting energy use."

The building is built around a covered courtyard but if the courtyard is fully covered with PV, it loses its daylighting and goes dark. They had to get the most efficient PV modules available to maximize energy production so they could leave openings over the courtyard to allow daylight into both the courtyard and the adjacent buildings.

"We added slots on the roof where the PV spans over the courtyard so some daylight could get in. The trick was putting the minimum amount of openings in the roof so we could generate the most electricity, but still allow enough daylight to enter the courtyard and the buildings so we could turn off the lights during the day," Kaneda explains.

"So we were balancing the structure, balancing the PV, balancing the daylighting and balancing the electric lighting and controls to optimize the overall building performance, but in this case the PVs and daylighting were really fighting against each other," says Kaneda.

Raising another challenge for Kaneda's team, Venter wanted the building to be resilient and able to operate off grid and without the use of diesel generators in case of a power outage.

"The easy way to do this would be to just put in a huge battery, but batteries contain materials that are bad for the environment plus they are really expensive," explains Kaneda. They decided instead to look at redesigning the system as a series of small PV systems, then getting a small battery bank sized to work with

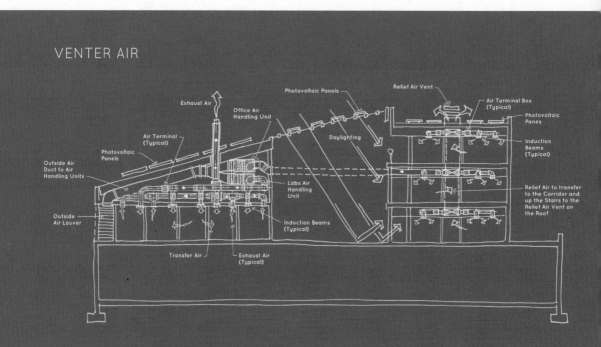

VENTER AIR

just one of the small PV systems. Depending on how much additional load you need to power the building in an emergency situation, a monitoring system could turn on additional PV systems to match the building load. Ideally, the system would be able to step up to 100 percent power on an as-needed basis.

The trouble is, someone would have to invent a system like this. A system that is able to step up power on demand does not exist, says Kaneda. So while the concept is innovative, the cost of designing a never before invented system like this was too great to implement on the JCVI building. "We don't always get to build what we come up with, but it was an interesting process figuring out a concept for a more resilient system," says Kaneda.

While the building is net zero, it uses the electrical grid as its "battery." An off the grid building might sound like it is the most green approach, but it isn't necessarily. "I really believe it's better for the environment to be able to dump extra clean energy back into the grid anyway," says Kaneda. "Pushing back excess energy onto the grid in the middle of a hot summer day allows the utility to use the excess clean energy to supply neighboring buildings, rather than importing dirty power from expensive and inefficient power plants that are only used when demand peaks."

To reduce energy use, JCVI conducted a plug load study that helped the lab optimize and reduce electricity use. JCVI incorporates ambient task lighting and LEDs and has some high-efficiency fluorescents, since it was designed just before LEDs became widely available. All occupied spaces receive natural light and fresh outside air ventilation; both increase comfort for the scientists.

The building and site also value water. Rainwater and air handler condensate will be collected and stored in a cistern, filtered, and then reused for non-potable purposes. The building includes waterless urinals and high-efficiency plumbing.

Working with a man like Dr. Venter and his team of incredibly innovative researchers makes for some unexpected diversions in the engineering process. For example, the scientists are trying to find, and in some cases engineer, microorganisms that can take waste and turn it into energy, thus cleaning the water for further use. The idea was to use some of the wastewater of the building in that research.

29

"One of the things that happened during the project is they said to us, 'pipe the urinals down to this special holding tank because we're looking to design a microbial fuel cell that both treats the waste and generates electricity,'" Rumsey recalls. "And we were like, what? OK, we'll do that. And then, three or four months later they said, 'OK, we figured that out, we now want the black water from the toilets down to a tank to see if we can treat that.' And so we redesigned the plumbing again. And then, they'd call again with another idea."

"We thought it was quite fascinating to provide these systems to help with their wastewater to energy research," says Rumsey. "It's such a great project and it is going to be one of those groundbreaking projects when it gets done."

"This lab can show people you don't have to just build a drab and boring box and super insulate it," says Principal John McDonald, who has done labs for almost twenty years and managed the JCVI Laboratory project for Intégral. Labs have often even been in basements, he says, but, "This building has great views, collaborative space for interaction, an open and free environment for information and knowledge and camaraderie, all in a net zero environment."

"We may not be able to take the design and put it in a completely different climate like Phoenix, Arizona," says McDonald "but we can apply the same process on other labs. It's a great model for high performing labs."

A Net Zero Museum

Groundbreaking, imaginative, innovative—another inspiring example of net zero on a massive scale is the Exploratorium Museum on San Francisco Bay, which Hydes calls "the most significant project we've done to date."

If you have a building that is sitting on a pier over the bay, why not use the bay water to cool the building? That's an imaginative question.

"This building is very imaginative, very innovative, and it's one of the first museums in the world to be net zero," says Rumsey, who along with his team, designed the system that uses the bay water underneath the pier it sits on to provide the cooling for the building's heat pump system. The building design incorporates in-slab radiant tubes, natural ventilation using 100 percent outdoor air, daylighting, and PV. The team designed it so no natural gas would be used for heating.

When they started on the project, about seven years ago, the sustainability goals were undefined. "So, we quietly designed the building in the background to be a very efficient building," recalls Rumsey. "We do that on all of our projects when we're working with an architect who is on board with that. We started to push internally for getting it really efficient and our team started looking at this building as if it were a net zero energy building."

The team started to bring up the net zero concept with the Exploratorium. They didn't jump up and down, "but as the project was progressing, so was the building industry and the idea of sustainability and the net zero energy concept," Rumsey says. (Now the net zero energy aspect of the museum has become an important part of the story of the new building and has even become part of the exhibits.)

Intégral designed the building so it would use half the energy as it would otherwise. "We had to do a lot of analysis to show that it made financial sense to do it this way, and it did," Rumsey comments.

The 1.2-megawatt rooftop PV system was one of the harder things to justify financially. It was originally a $10 million add-on. They considered getting third party financing for it, but the costs came down considerably during the time they worked on the building. They ended up working with PG&E because the utility offered big rebates for solar systems and energy efficiency to allow them to make the system affordable.

As a large public space, of course a museum's energy requirements are focused on heating and cooling, but the exhibits also take energy. "The exhibits have lights and motors and blowers and little pumps and a wide variety of little things that move stuff around, so we've started to talk to the exhibit designers about this net zero energy concept," Rumsey says. In fact, the design team conducted a study on lowering energy use of exhibits.

The word Exploratorium refers to innovation and creating new things. That's the theme of the museum and its exhibits. In a nice twist, some of the exhibits teach about the energy systems in the buildings. "It's a place where artists, engineers, scientists all come together to make the natural world compelling and understandable," explains Rumsey. "In the design, we've exposed some of the systems. There's a window on to the bay water cooling system and we've given them the information and opportunity to explain these things,

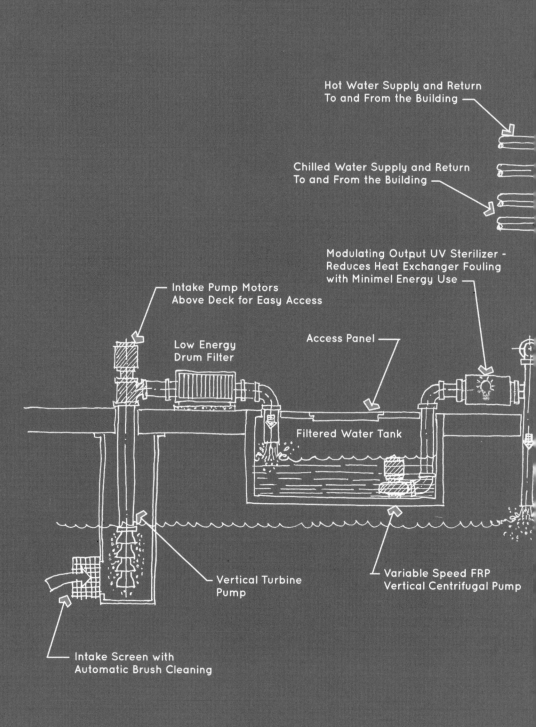

Hot Water Supply and Return
To and From the Building

Chilled Water Supply and Return
To and From the Building

Modulating Output UV Sterilizer -
Reduces Heat Exchanger Fouling
with Minimel Energy Use

Intake Pump Motors
Above Deck for Easy Access

Low Energy
Drum Filter

Access Panel

Filtered Water Tank

Vertical Turbine
Pump

Variable Speed FRP
Vertical Centrifugal Pump

Intake Screen with
Automatic Brush Cleaning

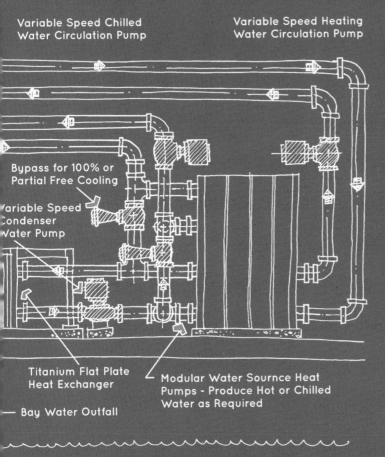

Variable Speed Chilled
Water Circulation Pump

Variable Speed Heating
Water Circulation Pump

Bypass for 100% or
Partial Free Cooling

Variable Speed
Condenser
Water Pump

Titanium Flat Plate
Heat Exchanger

Bay Water Outfall

Modular Water Sournce Heat
Pumps - Produce Hot or Chilled
Water as Required

EXPLORATORIUM - WATER

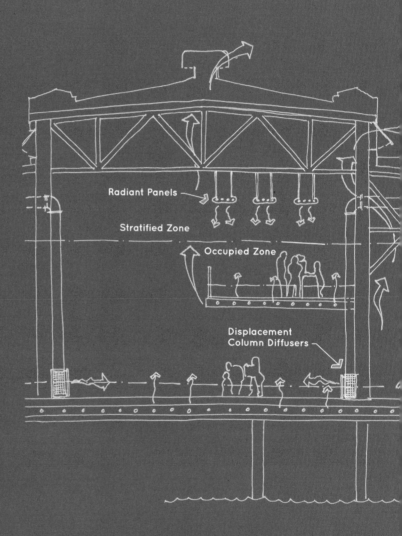

Radiant Panels

Stratified Zone

Occupied Zone

Displacement
Column Diffusers

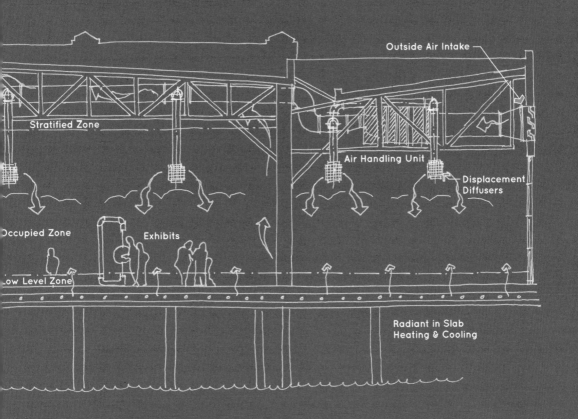

Outside Air Intake

Stratified Zone

Air Handling Unit

Displacement
Diffusers

Occupied Zone

Exhibits

Low Level Zone

Radiant in Slab
Heating & Cooling

and we're looking forward to the artists coming up with interpretations of what low energy means, the bay water system, the net zero approach, and I expect for years to come that there will be interesting interpretations of these things in their exhibits."

What the designers imagined happened, but only after diligent exploration and thanks to the unusual persistence and dedication of almost everyone involved, from the contractors to the client to the engineers and architects.

"It took a lot of time because we were doing something that's never been done in this way before—this bay water cooling system with heat pumps with no natural gas for heating, and radiant heating and cooling and no recirculated air," Rumsey explains. A few of the hurdles involved the complicated nature of a bay water system, meeting stringent regulations, re-building on a pier, and the fact that renovations are always more complicated than they first appear.

"There is a pier in San Francisco called Pier 1 that tried to use bay water cooling and it failed. So we looked at that building very closely and asked what went wrong, why did that system fail, and we learned from that. We spent a lot of time doing forensics on that building, and we decided the best way to approach this building is to pull in water in the same way that aquariums pull in water from a bay or body of water. They have to filter it and they have to do it in such a way that it doesn't hurt the marine life, and so we visited a variety of aquariums and we called people in Toronto and Hong Kong and all over the world trying to understand the best practices," recalls Rumsey.

Mussels and barnacles love attaching themselves to pipes when there is a lot of water flowing by. They just stick their receptacles out and grab plankton that's going by so they actually can grow better in a pipe than they would on a rock. "We have to have two pipes that we alternate back and forth on in order to always have a clean pipe and we used the shortest pipe possible so there's less pipe to clean, so we spent a lot of time figuring out things like that," says Rumsey.

It turns out the architect for the Exploratorium (EHDD Architects) was also the architect for Monterey Bay Aquarium. "At Monterey Bay they have a really good bay water system where they bring in lots of water for their exhibits. We spent a lot of time down there with them and we used the best practices from them and others to create a system that's very robust and environmentally sensitive," Rumsey says.

It's also a challenging environment to build in because there are about fifteen different agencies that oversee the bay plus some neighborhood associations who wanted to weigh in. The team followed Environmental Protection Agency guidelines about rejecting heat into bodies of water. They were written for large-scale power plants dumping huge quantities of heat into rivers, bays or the ocean. "We did a calculation that the amount of heat we are adding back into the water is less than the amount of heat the bay would absorb if the pier wasn't there and the sunlight were able to hit the bay. The quantity of heat we are rejecting is infinitesimal compared to a power plant. Nonetheless, we met all the requirements. But this added to the complication of the project to show we were meeting all the regulations," Rumsey explains.

"Everybody has put so much into this project because they all see it as one of the most significant projects on the West Coast. And a lot of us feel compelled on this project because we, as kids, went there, or our kids are going there now and there's nothing like going to a museum and seeing your kids get excited about understanding the world through these exhibits and through this experience."

"There are so many things about it that are so wonderful," Rumsey adds. "It looks great. It's a historic renovation, and it is going to inspire kids. Kids are going to learn from it. The biggest impact of that building is going to be their learning about net zero energy."

Like the VanDusen Botanical Gardens in Vancouver, perhaps one of the most innovative and beautiful buildings in the world, a Living Building that also embodies its mission in its structure and systems, this will be a truly inspiring place for millions of visitors. [See the Accelerate chapter to learn more about VanDusen.]

Special projects like VanDusen and the Exploratorium may not ever be copied exactly. They are unique. But Rumsey says, "The thing that is replicable is we can show that it is possible to do a 200,000-square foot net zero building, and there's this growing list of projects people can see, and there's going to be a certain point where people can no longer say, 'we can't do that.' And we need bigger and bigger examples."

VanDusen Botanical Garden Visitor Center,
Vancouver, British Columbia

The Largest Net Zero Office

The largest net zero office building is the National Renewable Energy Lab's Research Support Facility (RSF) in Golden, Colorado.

"What NREL was imagining they could do is build the largest zero energy building in the world and prove that it was cost effective," says Principal John Andary. The budget, as appropriated by Congress, was $254 per square foot for a 360,000-square-foot building.

"The project allowed me to imagine highest performance at the lowest cost," Andary adds. "I knew the design solution would have to be both an architectural solution and an engineering solution, and they had to be integrated in order for this all to happen at the lowest possible cost."

Andary worked at Stantec Engineering when he led the mechanical/electrical engineering team as well as the sustainable design and energy consulting effort on the RSF. Andary came to Intégral shortly after the RSF project when Intégral began work on NREL's next addition, a lab and data center. [See the Perform chapter to learn about the data center design.]

Andary considers himself a bioclimatic engineer. The term bioclimatic has traditionally been about passive architectural design that focuses on regionally appropriate comfort solutions. The imaginative question he asks on every project: "What if the passive architectural design is so good that the only mechanical system you need is one that provides clean and warm fresh air when the windows are closed? That can best be achieved through climate specific design and integration of passive architecture and active engineering systems."

"It also happens to be the most cost effective means of creating the healthiest possible buildings," he emphasizes.

While the building includes radiant slab for cooling and heating, and many other systems now common in net zero buildings, Andary likes to bring attention to this juncture where engineering and architecture cross, and focusing on that provides

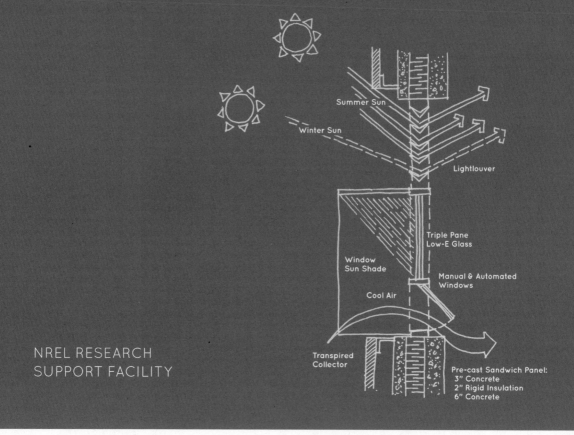

Summer Sun

Winter Sun

Lightlouver

Triple Pane
Low-E Glass

Window
Sun Shade

Manual & Automated
Windows

Cool Air

Transpired
Collector

Pre-cast Sandwich Panel:
3" Concrete
2" Rigid Insulation
6" Concrete

NREL RESEARCH
SUPPORT FACILITY

a little of the untold story of a building that has gotten a lot of press. (It was an AIA COTE Top Ten winner, and achieved the Award of Engineering Excellence from ASHRAE in 2012.)

The "cross" occurs in many common places in the design, such as solar orientation and the use of light shelves for daylighting. (One hundred percent of the spaces where people are working are daylit.) One juncture of architecture and engineering is a simple but powerful wall of exposed concrete Andary proposed. Walls are usually reserved for architects, but Andary thinks of the wall as part of the engineering. This kind of interior wall is normally used for cold storage buildings rather than offices. Made off site of concrete insulation and concrete, it has a high thermal mass and regulates the temperature in the building.

"We open the windows automatically at night and cool off all this concrete, and the next day it stays cool, and you can go through most of the year without requiring any cooling in a climate with normal summer high temperatures in the mid-90s F."

"It's like when you go into one of those old stone cathedrals on a hot day. The surfaces are cool from the previous night," he explains. "You've recreated the buildings of the past that have these massive walls and that can regulate their own temperature. That concrete sandwich panel wall is part of the mechanical system of the building and I knew it was cost-effective."

Andary and his team also capitalized on an opportunity underneath the building to take a similar passive approach to integrate the architecture and the engineering. Because of poor soil conditions, the building could not just sit on the concrete slab. It had to be lifted off the ground, which created a crawl space under the building. Here, Andary recommended what he calls a thermal labyrinth.

"We just had them [the architects] organize the structure they were making anyway as an air pathway, so at night we could draw cool air through here and cool off all this concrete," Andary explains. "Then the next day you just draw the hot air through there and the concrete cools it off and the building becomes its own air handler, but with no mechanical systems."

Andary also collaborated with the architect to use a transpired solar collector as both a mechanical and an architectural feature on the front of the building. Again, this is an atypical application; collectors like this are more typically used in warehouse buildings and hidden from view. The sun heats the surface of the dark metal collector on the south side of the building and air gets drawn through the perforations and passively heated. This is a very inexpensive way to provide heat, and with no fossil fuel.

In the winter, the heat off these transpired collectors goes to heat the labyrinth in the crawl space. Now there is a big data center that has been added in the building that pumps out heat all the time. In the winter, waste heat from the data center also dumps down into the labyrinth and heats up that concrete. The system uses the warm concrete to warm the air that comes into the building the next day.

"This is actually architectural, structural engineering and mechanical engineering all coming together in an integrated way and a cost effective way because we already had to build the building this way to reduce the energy use and make it perform better," says Andary. This is how engineering meets bioclimatic design.

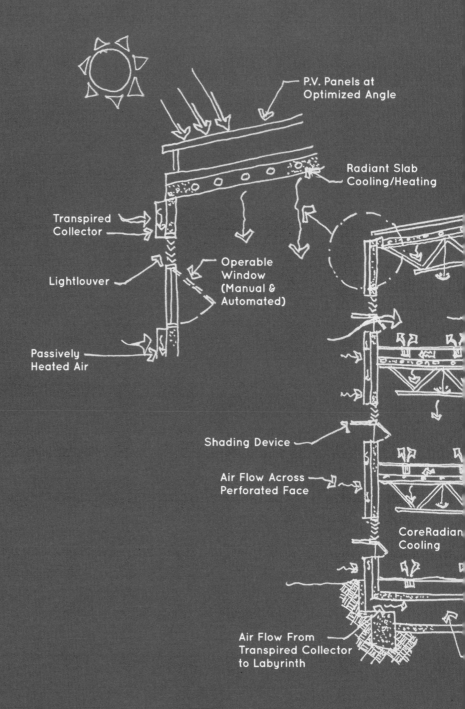

P.V. Panels at
Optimized Angle

Radiant Slab
Cooling/Heating

Transpired
Collector

Operable
Window
(Manual &
Automated)

Lightlouver

Passively
Heated Air

Shading Device

Air Flow Across
Perforated Face

CoreRadiant
Cooling

Air Flow From
Transpired Collector
to Labyrinth

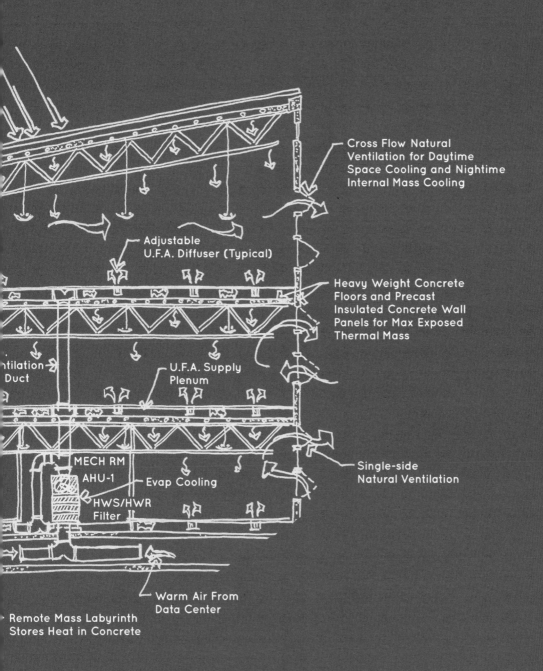

Cross Flow Natural
Ventilation for Daytime
Space Cooling and Nightime
Internal Mass Cooling

Adjustable
U.F.A. Diffuser (Typical)

Heavy Weight Concrete
Floors and Precast
Insulated Concrete Wall
Panels for Max Exposed
Thermal Mass

...ntilation
Duct

U.F.A. Supply
Plenum

MECH RM
AHU-1
Evap Cooling

Single-side
Natural Ventilation

HWS/HWR
Filter

Warm Air From
Data Center

Remote Mass Labyrinth
Stores Heat in Concrete

43

The Grand Mosque

It takes imagination and innovation to achieve net zero and regenerative buildings, especially on a large scale, but engineering needs to be about much more than energy. It needs to be about people.

If millions of people are kneeling on the floor in prayer, what if we cool the floor rather than the air above them? What if we also ventilate from the floor where the people are? These are the imaginative questions Principal Tom Simpson asked as he worked in a challenging and hot climate to retrofit the Grand Mosque in Mecca. These ideas could save energy and, perhaps more importantly, they could provide comfort to millions of pilgrims and prevent the spread of disease.

The client was King Abdullah in Saudi Arabia, who wanted to double the size of Mecca's Grand Mosque to accommodate more pilgrims and provide more support service space. (Every Muslim is encouraged to make a pilgrimage to Mecca at least once in a lifetime.) The addition to the mosque added about 3 million square feet of space to accommodate another 560,000 people. "It's like six of the biggest football stadiums in the United States, filled with people from all walks of life, speaking all languages, from all over the world," Simpson explains. Accommodating them has to do with safety, health and comfort. The potential and the challenge was huge.

Simpson met Intégral's Trevor Butler for the first time in an elevator on his way to the project kickoff meeting in Cairo. (You can't go to Mecca unless you are Muslim, so the meetings were held in Cairo.)

Intégral was hired to be part of the sustainability team. "Their religious beliefs very much focus on the environment and water. Water is holy on that site," explains Simpson. So sustainability is spiritual, in this case.

"Mosque issues are water, cooling and ventilation," explains Butler, who works all over the world but is based out of Intégral's Kelowna, B.C. office. The pilgrims need lots of water on site for ceremonial use, plus they have over a million people flushing toilets. To handle the huge water consumption at the mosque the

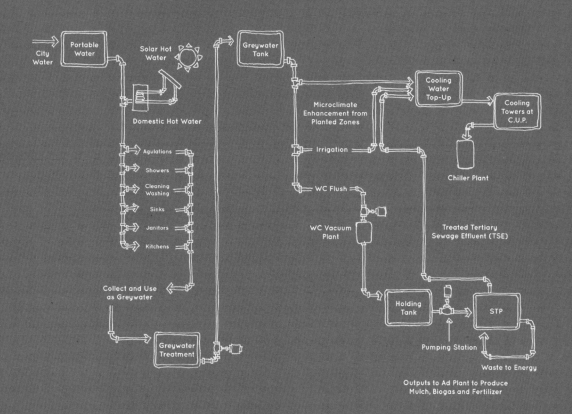

City Water

Portable Water

Solar Hot Water

Domestic Hot Water

Agulations
Showers
Cleaning Washing
Sinks
Janitors
Kitchens

Collect and Use as Greywater

Greywater Treatment

Greywater Tank

Microclimate Enhancement from Planted Zones

Irrigation

WC Flush

WC Vacuum Plant

Cooling Water Top-Up

Cooling Towers at C.U.P.

Chiller Plant

Treated Tertiary Sewage Effluent (TSE)

Holding Tank

Pumping Station

STP

Waste to Energy

Outputs to Ad Plant to Produce Mulch, Biogas and Fertilizer

GRAND MOSQUE - WATER FLOW

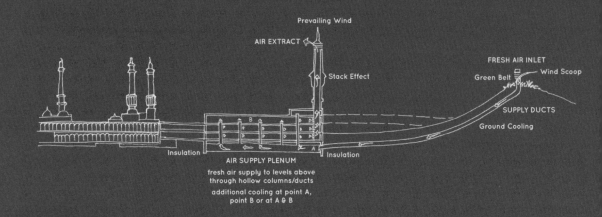

GRAND MOSQUE – AIR OPTION 1

sustainability team recommended installing vacuum toilets, which use one-fifth of the water. This would save 80 percent of the water consumed from energy intensive desalination plants located kilometers away.

According to Butler, other sustainable design questions included: How enclosed can we make the new prayer halls and still have the pilgrims be safe? How do we get fresh air in and to the people in such a giant place?

With more than a million people and located in this climate, the mosque is very, very hot. The new prayer halls were going to add roughly 70,000 tons of air conditioning. "That's right, 70,000 tons," Simpson emphasizes. "Through the process we came up with a strategy that would reduce that to 30,000 tons." That's an incredible reduction in environmental impact.

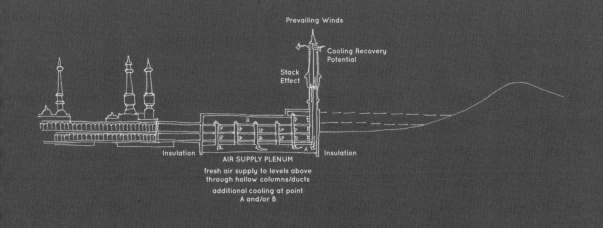

Prevailing Winds

Cooling Recovery Potential

Stack Effect

B

A

Insulation

Insulation

AIR SUPPLY PLENUM

fresh air supply to levels above
through hollow columns/ducts

additional cooling at point
A and/or B

GRAND MOSQUE – AIR OPTION 2

The subject of Butler's doctoral dissertation is earth coupled ventilation systems, aka earth tubes, which he proposed for the mosque. Earth tubes are buried horizontally two meters deep and provide air with no compressor and no refrigerant. They provide a completely passive way of cooling. Butler is writing about how to design and install them to help people avoid putting that chiller on the roof. Earth tubes are just about the most imaginative and most perfectly suited technology for bringing fresh air into a building like a mosque in Mecca. "The Chinese and Middle Easterners have used them for centuries. Now we are rediscovering old techniques that worked extremely effectively before modern technology was invented," says Butler.

The process for designing the addition and its systems worked like this. The King formed a committee of representatives from the Ministry of Higher Education in Saudi Arabia. The design build team included the Ministry, a contractor, and the design team.

"The process was very interesting," says Simpson a bit ironically. "Mechanical engineers were meeting separately, plumbing engineers were meeting about

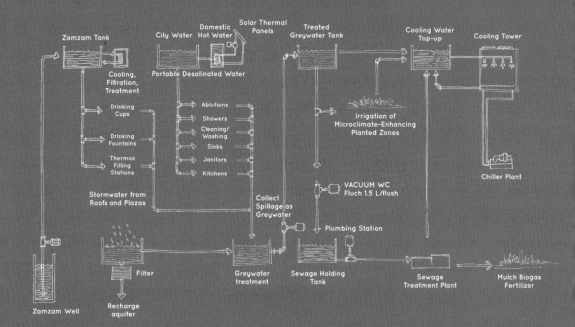

Zamzam Tank

Cooling,
Filtration,
Treatment

Drinking
Cups

Drinking
Fountains

Thermos
Filling
Stations

Stormwater from
Roofs and Plazas

Zamzam Well

Filter

Recharge
aquifer

City Water

Domestic
Hot Water

Solar Thermal
Panels

Portable Desalinated Water

Ablutions

Showers

Cleaning/
Washing

Sinks

Janitors

Kitchens

Collect
Spillage as
Greywater

Greywater
treatment

Treated
Greywater Tank

Irrigation of
Microclimate-Enhancing
Planted Zones

VACUUM WC
Fluch 1.5 L/flush

Plumbing Station

Sewage Holding
Tank

Sewage
Treatment Plant

Cooling Water
Top-up

Cooling Tower

Chiller Plant

Mulch Biogas
Fertilizer

GRAND MOSQUE - WATER

plumbing only, there was an architectural meeting, a civil engineer meeting was being held separately, and the sustainability committee was meeting." Simpson was attending all the meetings and attempting to convey information across the disparate groups.

"The process was lacking the discussion and consensus building that comes from an integrated design process," according to Simpson, and he suggested that they needed fewer meetings and more representatives at one table. And they listened. The separate committee meetings turned into an integrated meeting and the results were dramatic.

"We sat down in a small room with the civil engineers, the structural engineers, the mechanical and electrical engineers and the architects and we decided how we were going to move air through that building without using ductwork. We worked on how to improve indoor air quality for the people who were coming there because potential spread of disease was a big challenge. We agreed to introduce the air from the floor so people could breathe it low down before it picked up the contaminants from the people."

The prayer halls are quite tall. The integrated team proposed radiant floor cooling to cool people directly rather than cooling the air. They worked together to come up with a strategy to improve comfort and air quality and drastically reduce energy. "It was a really elegant and neat solution," recalls Simpson.

"We had a great strategy. We were using the structure to distribute air. We were going to use radiant cooling, desiccant systems and earth tubes to pre-cool the high volume of ventilation air. We were driving the energy down between 50-60 percent with these proposed solutions," he says.

The project had a very accelerated completion requirement and was fast-tracked. It was completed in approximately twelve months, according to DLB Associates, the engineering firm that installed the central cooling plant. In the end the schedule became the most important thing and forced a traditional mechanical system solution.

"But we did show them a different process," Simpson adds optimistically. Success is hard to measure in this project, but the potential for serving humanity and providing a healthy and comfortable prayer environment for millions of pilgrims through imaginative approaches in design is worthy, as worthy as the potential for energy savings and reducing environmental impact, and provides a great model for innovative approaches to future projects.

Success in Mecca ended up being more about transforming minds and processes than the end product. The proposed solutions might have been monumental, but changing a thinking process and demonstrating integrated design and collaboration is not a failure of imagination.

Innovation begins with a hunger—a yearning for some kind of change. To innovate successfully in any field, first you have to care. You have to start by asking: Why can't things be different? And then, you ask how... how do we begin to change? You can pursue sustainable design because it is rational. You can pursue it because it improves humanity's place within our built and natural environment. And if you are concerned about the future, you believe we must pursue sustainable design because lives may depend on it.

"Even if every single building were a LEED Platinum building, we are still on a collision course with the planet's ability to sustain us," contends McLennan.

"Our climate is going to change and it's going to have a significant impact," comments Intégral Principal Bungane Mehlomakulu. "From this point forward it's reducing that impact as much as possible. From an engineering point of view, from an inertia standpoint, there's just far too much inertia in the wrong direction for us to overcome in a short period of time."

Mehlomakulu thinks back on days as a child in summer camp in the wilderness of Canada, near where he grew up in Toronto. These summers in nature influenced him to work toward reducing the impact of the built environment. "I really had this feeling I wanted nature to be here for my kids' kids. I want them to be able to experience the world as I do. But I don't think they will."

At school, Mehlomakulu, who recently completed an MBA in Sustainable Systems at Bainbridge Graduate Institute, has heard the word "apocaloptimist" tossed around in discussions about maintaining hope and purpose while facing the inevitability of climate change, population increases and environmental degradation. He explains the simple definition: "Basically the whole world is going to hell, but you think it's going to be okay."

McLennan doesn't particularly like the word but seems to agree with the spirit: "While it is easy to feel defeated and pessimistic by the overwhelming evidence of energy and water scarcity, climate change and worldwide economic upheaval, I consider it more useful to look at these significant challenges as opportunities to re-imagine civilization in a way that ensures our long-term place in it."

"Every building for me is something I am going to leave on the earth once I am gone. I want to feel that I did something on this planet for the next generation," comments Vancouver Principal Goran Ostojic.

"Sometimes it's easier to go the simpler route or to give up," he says, "but then I think 'if you don't do it, you will miss that opportunity to do the best you can and push the limit.' With every building we work on, even if it's just one building at a time, if we reduce the energy use by 50 percent, it's a huge game changer."

This kind of attitude is how we end up with wonderful buildings, so inspiring, worthy of copying, worthy of scaling up—even those that end up differently than we imagine. They set new standards because someone asks: How will this building's shape change the light? How can we capitalize on the bay air? How will this glass feel for the person who is sitting here? How will this system sound? How does runoff change the ecosystem around us? Can it feed a green roof? How do I work with people? Am I in a box or a silo? What does collaboration mean? Can we work shoulder to shoulder on this design? Can children learn from this place? Can it cause inhabitants to be more creative and innovative? Can it keep people from getting sick? Does it inspire people? How does it connect to the earth?

"The built environment shapes and influences what we do and how we behave. And how we are able to change the built environment influences how we change our behavior," reflects Mehlomakulu.

Buildings can be standard, or they can be transformational. The difference is imagination.

PERFORM

02

Attitude is the biggest driver behind successful high-performance projects.

— Greg Franta, FAIA

Perform

Opening a window, lowering a shade, these once ordinary "controls" still create more comfort and efficiency than many new technologies we add to our buildings.

High performance engineering and design may have connotations of bells and whistles and gadgets, and extremely sophisticated machinery and systems. While advances in technology—particularly for a few items like solar panels, glazing, LEDs and dashboards—do play an important role in achieving higher performance, if we start with energy savings and work our way to occupant comfort, passive design strategies remain the unsexy but fundamental pillars of performance.

Many of Intégral's clients understand this and that is what makes them, and their buildings, exceptional, according to Hydes. "The issue of avoiding air conditioning and using more passive systems is fundamental to much of our work in the past two decades," he comments.

Solar, passive design, efficient envelopes, radiant slab and chilled beams, heat recovery, daylighting, natural ventilation, on-site water capture and treatment —these are some of the main designs and systems we think of as innovative in green design, but most go back to the Romans or earlier and have been a pretty common part of design in Europe and Asia for some time.

We have proven we can build small and large net zero buildings using mostly low-tech techniques and systems. We're starting to build Living Buildings and Living Communities using new combinations of mostly the same passive strategies that have worked for centuries. So the challenge is not necessarily inventing new systems, it's getting them installed in larger buildings and in more buildings and on a larger neighborhood scale.

"When I awarded the certification plaques on the LEED buildings when I served as USGBC chair I would say, 'This is the worst this building should ever perform for the rest of its life.' We should be committed to long-term continuous improvement. That's why at Intégral we pledge to reduce our energy and waste by 20 percent over the next two years as a company. We have really deep green offices at Intégral, and we believe they can get even better now that they are built. We hope to do the same with all our clients' buildings."

– Kevin Hydes, Founder and CEO Intégral Group

So, what's holding us back? The story of high performance must start with what's broken in standard design. By far the biggest issue is still oversizing systems like chillers and pumps, which usually should not only be smaller, but often times may be completely eliminated. Integrated design remains disintegrated for the most part. We still suffer greatly from the "we've always done it that way" (since World War II, at least) approach and we're slowed by fear of the unknown among public officials, building owners and design teams. These are essentially the same obstacles green building proponents have been up against for years.

On the bright side, enough green design elements in engineering have been built that engineers running into these same obstacles can do what Hydes and others do when they want to challenge the standard way of doing things: Walk the building owners over and show them the chilled beam system in a nearby building. Bring in the contractor who installed a recent radiant slab and let her talk to the team. Use analysis to prove the efficiency and savings through models.

"Proposing chilled beams in the Cal Poly Science building was not just innovative, but people saw it as a little crazy for a lab. But we had experience doing it and

> "When you first start off trying to solve a problem, the first solutions you come up with are very complex, and most people stop there. But if you keep going, and live with the problem and peel more layers of the onion off, you can often times arrive at some very elegant and simple solutions. Most people just don't put in the time or energy to get there."
>
> – Steve Jobs

we were able to point to that," recalls Principal Tyler Bradshaw. Not only did the chilled beams go in, they were actually cheaper than the conventional system.

We have a new incentive now for sustainable design, even if energy stays cheap enough to waste. Now we have carbon, something Europeans have also been designing against for some time. Designing to lower greenhouse gas emissions has huge potential for immediately reducing environmental impact without anyone having to develop any new technology to save us from ourselves. Carbon should become a new driver of high-performance design in these times.

For example, Intégral's COO, Conrad Schartau, used a variety of passive and innovative refrigeration techniques to massively reduce emissions in a Wal-Mart store in Burlington, Ontario. One of the first pumped secondary carbon dioxide refrigeration systems in Canada, it was also much less costly than one using a standard refrigeration system.

"A standard refrigerant, say 404A, is 3992 times more harmful to the planet, to the ozone layer for the same amount of mass," Schartau explains. "It's massive because up to 33 percent of any charge that's in a supermarket refrigeration system historically will leak. Every supermarket refrigeration system in North America has 3000 pounds of refrigerant. That means 1000 pounds of refrigerant is released to the atmosphere."

An additional bonus with this kind of system is cost. The cost of a pound of 404 is a probably about $25. And the cost of a pound of CO_2: "I'd be lying if it's a dollar," Schartau says. "CO_2 is cheap; it's got an ozone depletion potential of zero and a global warming potential of one."

This and other energy choices, particularly around lighting, make the store 56 percent more efficient than the standard Wal-Mart store. Since Wal-Mart has about 6400 stores in North America, Schartau says, the implications for reduced emissions, if replicated, could be enormous. And it is being replicated, he says.

"It wouldn't sound like much in the United Kingdom," where they have done many similar systems, reflects Schartau.

REFRIGERATION SYSTEM

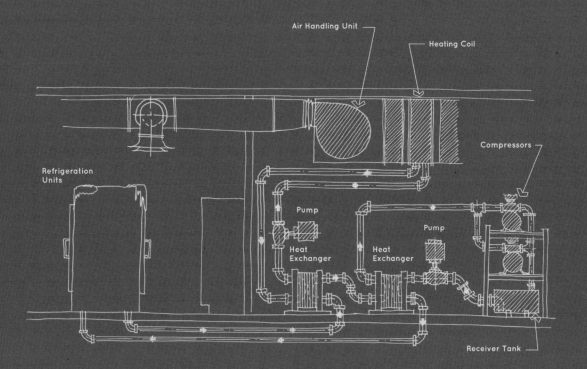

McDonell agrees: Innovation like this and like chilled beams and radiant slabs is not a stretch; it's the education that's hard. "Leading-edge designers will all say, we already know what should be done and how it works and how to make it work properly; it's convincing everybody else on the team that we can do it," says McDonell. "That's still the biggest, hardest challenge of all these buildings." Once you propose something that isn't standard, he says, "Now you are under a microscope. Now you're the guy who is taking responsibility for this so-called new fangled radiant slab system or geo-exchange heat pump or whatever it is. And you have to work harder and be more resourceful to prove yourself and your ideas, even if tried and true across Europe. You might, for example, even have to go down to the plant room and watch the installation of the pipes until you see them installed correctly."

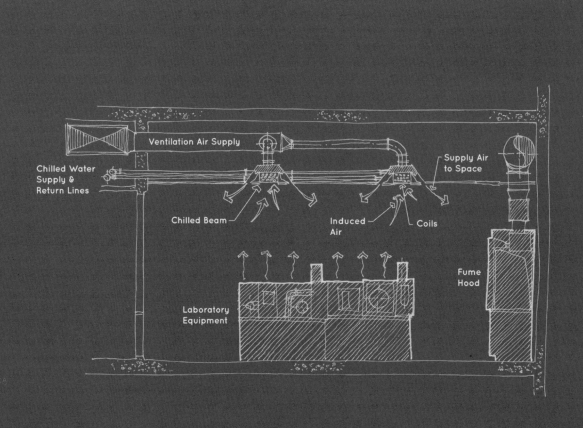

Ventilation Air Supply

Chilled Water
Supply &
Return Lines

Supply Air
to Space

Chilled Beam

Induced
Air

Coils

Fume
Hood

Laboratory
Equipment

CHILLED BEAM

Fighting Friction

In the energy efficiency retrofit of the Oakland Museum, Rumsey's team did just that. "We did the drawing for the contractor to use for installation and it showed smooth pipes. But the contractor put the elbows in even though they weren't in the drawing because that's the way they had always done it," Rumsey says. So, Rumsey's team knew they had to go watch the pipes being installed to make sure they followed the drawings.

"We were down in the plant room and we kept talking with them and finally the general contractor asked: 'You're not asking us to build these pipes like a sewer pipe are you?' And we said, 'Yes! Actually, we are.' And so they made the leap and they were able to install smooth pipes and follow the drawing.

"Pipes are powerful. This is simple Victorian engineering. In older buildings, they had to have bigger pipes because they didn't have pumps and fans," according to Rumsey.

"If everybody got this, we could reduce electricity use on a massive scale," Rumsey points out, while standing under the straight pipes in the museum's mechanical room with a group of Intégral's junior engineers. "If you have the right size (bigger) pipe, you can get rid of pumps," he tells them. There's a well-known photo of Rumsey there in the Oakland Museum mechanical room crouching next to a pile of pumps he found unnecessary. In a nod to his mentor Amory Lovins, who coined the term "negawatts," Rumsey calls the uninstalled pumps "negapumps."

In another case Rumsey's team put in a chiller for a high school and they used smooth pipes and small pumps. The school turned on the chiller and it didn't work. The contractor immediately said, "The pump is too small." So Rumsey got a call from the school principal.

"It's been a long time since I got called in by the principal," he laughs. "In fact, the chiller was air locked. They hadn't purged the air. So, we purged it and the chiller was actually getting 20 percent more air, so it was working even more efficiently than we expected. The contractor just automatically assumed it was the pump because he had never before seen a small pump on a system like this."

Doug Kerr at Elementa, Intégral's London office, agrees that when facilities teams don't operate a system correctly, it's the system that immediately gets a bad reputation, creating more challenges for anyone who proposes it later.

"We often use underfloor heating (radiant slab) in schools," he recounts. "In a couple of cases, the kids come in in the morning and they say, 'It's freezing cold.'"

With radiant, you ramp down through the night, but it never truly goes off, he explains. "What we're finding is the caretaker (often called the janitor in North America), is used to coming in and turning the boilers off every night because that's what they used to do. In the morning, he comes in and turns it on, but it's got a three-hour lag. And so there's nothing wrong with the system, it's a great system. It's education that is the barrier.

"But the problem is, it can very quickly get bad press. 'Oh, that's a bad system. That doesn't work. I've got a teacher friend who works over in that school and it's freezing.'"

So it's also about evangelism, Kerr says. "That's the thing about sustainability. There's an element of evangelism, but it's got to be married to practical use. As engineers, when we're talking about systems, we need to make sure we show the entire picture. You need knowledgeable people running the building and you must share the information."

In the Tahoe Center for Environmental Science, one of the first LEED Platinum labs and the first lab to used chilled beams, the team had to explain what chilled beams were. They did a cost assessment half way through and a chiller was on the costs sheet. "We said, 'We don't need a chiller,'" Rumsey recalls. "They took it out, but later we saw that they put it back in. They just couldn't get used to this idea that you could build a lab building without a chiller."

This is one of the barriers to achieving high performance. The contractor was convinced the system they proposed would not work because the contractor was not familiar with chilled beams. "We didn't get approval for eliminating the chiller until the end phase of design," Rumsey says. "The moral of the story: It doesn't take longer to build a low energy building. It takes longer to get everybody on board."

Another of the barriers to innovation is fear of the unknown," says Bradshaw. "Fear is how we ended up with a double-sided building in India." [See the story of Infosys in the Accelerate chapter.]

"THAT'S THE THING ABOUT SUSTAINABILITY. THERE'S AN ELEMENT OF EVANGELISM, BUT IT'S GOT TO BE MARRIED TO PRACTICAL USE. AS ENGINEERS, WHEN WE'RE TALKING ABOUT SYSTEMS, WE NEED TO MAKE SURE WE SHOW THE ENTIRE PICTURE. YOU NEED KNOWLEDGEABLE PEOPLE RUNNING THE BUILDING AND YOU MUST SHARE THE INFORMATION."

WATERLESS URINAL

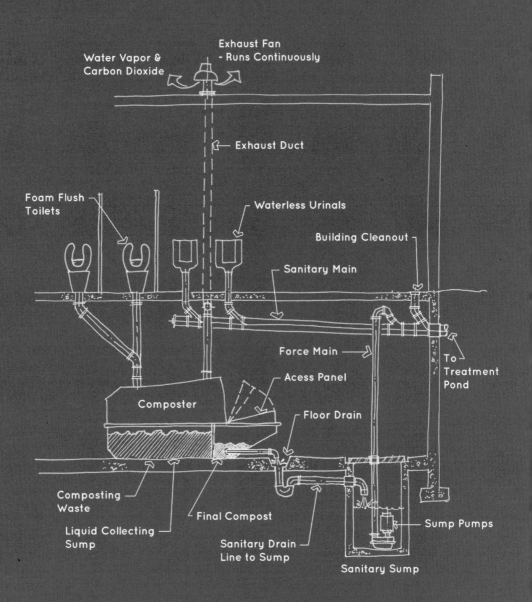

Water Vapor &
Carbon Dioxide

Exhaust Fan
- Runs Continuously

Exhaust Duct

Foam Flush
Toilets

Waterless Urinals

Building Cleanout

Sanitary Main

Force Main

Acess Panel

To
Treatment
Pond

Composter

Floor Drain

Composting
Waste

Final Compost

Sump Pumps

Liquid Collecting
Sump

Sanitary Drain
Line to Sump

Sanitary Sump

Plumbing issues in particular raise people's most base fears about health issues or perhaps it's possible to exploit people's base fears around health issues to protect business. In some cases, people have even been known to try to unfairly affiliate the spread of deadly contagious disease such as SARS with the use of waterless urinals.

Associate Principal Susan Ecker recalls her fight to get waterless urinals accepted in the City of Oakland starting in 2006. "We met with building officials and they were reluctant to allow waterless urinals even though over thirty jurisdictions in the state of California allowed the installation of waterless urinals via the Alternative Materials and Methods Request (AMMR) process. We provided documentation showing that the U.S. Army Corps of Engineers and the California Division of the State Architect allowed the use of waterless urinals."

Waterless urinals were finally included in the California Plumbing Code in 2010.

Similarly, she says, "Rainwater catchment systems for use inside the building for flushing water closets is not even in the code, so we have to prepare an AMMR and provide it to the Authority Having Jurisdiction in order to gain approval on a case by case basis." Despite the extra effort, Ecker has worked on rainwater catchment systems on a number of her projects.

"Water is such a critical issue, but it's still cheap so it's hard to get people to focus on it as much as energy," says Ecker. "Water is actually the most vital of natural resources simply because we cannot live without water," she explains. "An average adult can survive only about a week without water. Clean drinking water is taken for granted in the United States. Many places in the world have limited access to clean drinking water."

However, more and more states at least have guidelines for things like graywater, blackwater and rainwater catchment systems, and with droughts gripping the West and companies like Google possibly aiming for a net zero water campus where all on-site water is captured, treated and reused, water will someday soon take its rightful place alongside energy as a resource worth protecting.

The Character of Innovation

Change water codes, watch installations, go back to the drawing board and take the chiller out until it stays out, challenge the standard way of doing things. This approach isn't for every engineer. Innovation, achieving high performance, is character driven more than technology driven. To achieve innovation, the role of the engineer and his or her relationship to the building owner, design team and occupant needs to be different than it traditionally has been.

"Engineering, by definition, was a more narrowly defined field and now what's required is a much more expansive view, and so you have engineers getting into other roles and other realms because of how they think as opposed to what they think. There's a blurring of the edges and it's not so formulaic," says McLennan.

"My wife and kids say I am a dork engineer," comments Principal John McDonald, "but I'm not a typical engineer because I am always asking questions, like 'what color are you going to paint the space? Do you have enough white board space?' Things you normally wouldn't associate with engineering."

"Some architects don't like it when I ask...and some do. I like the architects who ask the mechanical questions, like Jon Schleuning and Tim Evans with SRG out of Portland. We can have these really wide-ranging conversations."

When Schleuning, Evans, and McDonald worked together on the Health Sciences Surge Building for University of California, Riverside, Schleuning wanted to create a corner, with books and couches so people would collaborate. "We wanted ventilation with outside air," recalls McDonald. "So we came up with a room like a lanai, a Hawaiian outdoor room." This beautiful and creative solution came from two people crossing into each other's disciplines as they collaborated. It came from a blurring of the edges.

"You can't just innovate in terms of the buildings and the systems, you have to innovate as a profession. You have to innovate as an engineer, as a person," says McLennan.

"Whether it's the type of projects we get engaged with or the roles we play in projects, this constant expansion provides new opportunities to learn and helps us to become better."

"I practiced with both Peter and Kevin when they were competitors," McLennan recounts, "and they often played that expanded role, acting as direct advisors to clients, participating with the architect in the design process outside of engineering."

A lot of innovation is about communication, relationships and character says Hydes. "Peter has just one little sheet of paper he uses when he talks to clients. And it's incredibly powerful." The sheet of paper no doubt has innovative solutions written on it but the powerful part is in the way he communicates the ideas.

Health Sciences Surge Building, UC Riverside

"There's a little bit that is sort of bordering on evangelical, but not quite," Hydes explains, echoing Kerr. It's often about listening. "If we go to meetings and just pound our fist, we're not going to get anywhere. We go, we listen, we share, we encourage, and then, when we need to, we urge. Knowing when to move from listener to leader, and vice versa, that's the absolute skill. If you can get that right, you can get great things to happen."

For example, Hydes tells a story of a project he worked on in Egypt where he decided to shift his approach. "We were doing a building in Cairo and we wanted to propose radiant slab. I was in a presentation with the team and the client and I'm standing up there with some diagrams to advocate for it. I didn't even get half way through my first sentence when this guy interrupts me and says, with his arms folded, a big Egyptian guy, he says: 'Every pipe in Cairo leaks.'

"And I thought, well I'll ignore this for a second. And I tried to talk and he says, 'Every pipe in Cairo leaks.' And I thought, who is this guy?

"Well, he's an engineer and a really smart engineer and he's worked in Egypt most of his career. And, I finally got it. If he tells me every pipe in Cairo leaks, then I've got to believe it because I've never lived in Cairo. So, his point was obvious, why would you put a pile of pipes in the middle of a slab when we haven't got a plumber in Cairo who can stop a leak?

"So, we shifted. I called Peter and said, 'We've got a problem,' and he said, 'Put a Thermafuser in.' And so we still ended up with a pretty efficient building but without any pipes that were leaking. So, you look at what I could have done there. I could have argued and questioned but why would you argue with somebody from that place who knows?"

Listening is the key to tailoring a message, says Bradshaw. "Some audiences (schools, government buildings) really care about climate change. They know about global warming. You can pitch the environment to this client.

"Projects all have different drivers and some clients may not be as motivated by global warming. For this audience I say, 'this will lower your operating costs, lower

RADIANT HEATING & COOLING

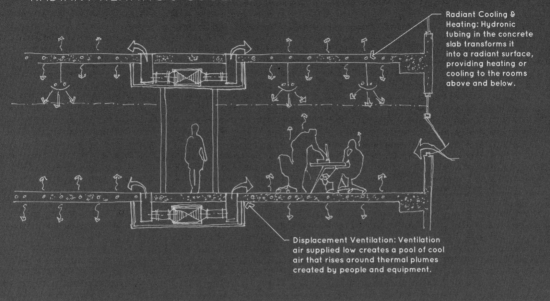

Radiant Cooling & Heating: Hydronic tubing in the concrete slab transforms it into a radiant surface, providing heating or cooling to the rooms above and below.

Displacement Ventilation: Ventilation air supplied low creates a pool of cool air that rises around thermal plumes created by people and equipment.

your energy use,' and I provide more of a financial analysis. Anything that has a return on investment of six years or less, they'll often do it," Bradshaw says.

Getting sustainability and energy efficiency measures included is not always about pitching. Sometimes you can just do it. "You don't necessarily need a green client to do green stuff," McDonald says. "You might as well replace equipment with more efficient equipment. If you have to replace air handlers anyway, you can use one with a larger cross section to lower the air velocity and the extra cost of a more efficient piece of equipment is negligible."

Intégral HR Director Maria Briggs Berta seeks out and hires people like McDonald and Bradshaw. "These engineers are different from engineers at standard firms," she says. "These engineers have to go out to the clients and they have to convince the clients that it's worth taking a risk. They have to instill trust. They have to instill enthusiasm and passion. Our competitive edge is going after people with passion."

"We really need different perspectives," she says "and we are looking for that person who is not afraid to take a risk and is going to be pushing the envelope. So there's a lot more that our engineers need to do because we're interested in people who want to go out and change the way the world builds buildings."

Diversity Adds to Innovation

The character of innovation relies on different ways of thinking, and a homogenous group is not going to provide that.

"If we were homogeneous here, then we would all just settle into our groove. But if you are working next to somebody who is different from you, that's a challenge. It's intriguing and you sort of broaden your horizons and it adds to fulfillment in the workplace," says Berta.

Yet architecture and engineering firms are not particularly diverse. If you have an all Caucasian office you are probably missing out on some different ways of approaching problems than if you had a more ethnically diverse firm, says McLennan, adding, "Out of all the professions, this is also one of the least gender diverse. So it's a profession that needs to change more significantly."

"If you go in an office where it's only 10 percent women, it discourages some women," McLennan says. "They don't have the role models or people in leadership that they can relate to. But, when you look at the leading engineers in the sustainability field, a higher percentage of them are women."

"Women have been key in sustainability," comments Principal Lisa Fay Matthiessen. "Women have gotten interested in sustainability because it's collaborative, filled with passion and values-driven. A lot of the men involved in sustainability are that way too—more collaborative, more passionate, more in it for moral or philosophical rewards than for the money."

According to a study Matthiessen cites that looked at Fortune 500 companies, if a company has three or more women on the board, the company's financial success is dramatically higher. "It's not because you put the women there, but the women being there is a reflection of other things the firm is doing right. It's the indicator of good policy and collaboration and all those other things," she explains.

Some of the best and greenest architectural firms have created telecommuting, flex-time and parental leave policies to try to recruit and maintain women in

"YOU HAVE TO SEEK WOMEN OUT AND LOOK AT HOW YOU ARE STRUCTURED AS A FIRM, WHAT KIND OF POLICIES YOU HAVE—TELECOMMUTING, FLEX-TIME, PARENTAL LEAVE— YOU HAVE TO CONSCIOUSLY ARRANGE HIERARCHIES AND TEAMS TO BE COLLABORATIVE. MAKE IT HAPPEN."

leadership roles; the combination of passion and idealism in the work and the conscious effort to create work/life balance attracts the best and the brightest. "The funny thing is that once these policies are in place, it turns out the young men in the office are all over it. They just love it," Matthiessen comments. "Google and some of the companies that are becoming really successful now have more of a collaborative model, and they deliberately structure themselves to achieve this."

"As far as people from other cultures, you go to a USGBC conference, it's pretty much white and pretty much American," she observes. "We really need to work on that. I'm totally in the camp that you need to consciously place diverse people in leadership roles. Some firms deliberately place women in key positions on every project team; this radically changes the dynamic of the team. You have to seek women out and look at how you are structured as a firm, what kind of policies you have—telecommuting, flex-time, parental leave—you have to consciously arrange hierarchies and teams to be collaborative. Make it happen."

Analysis is Intuitive

Innovative engineering may require new roles and new relationships. It may require emotional intelligence, character, ability to listen, diversity, and about a million "soft" skills. But innovative engineering still requires good old-fashioned math. Kim Traber and Neil Bulger will argue that even analysis is more about intuition than math, but building owners and architects really like to see the numbers.

Analysis and energy modeling not only create options for design but can also be the most influential evidence-based argument for doing more innovative designs and for investing in sustainability.

In the case of convincing data center owners and operators to consider energy efficiency, it required both persistence and data. Data centers are some of the largest energy users and traditionally have massive cooling systems that consume as much electricity as the computers they serve. In 2003, Rocky Mountain Institute held a charrette in San Jose on data centers, and the question emerged: Why not bring in outside air to cool the building? Peter Rumsey and his analysis team were there. At the time, airside economizing in data centers was a rare thing and the idea seemed a little frightening, according to Traber.

"The resistance to airside economizing in data centers, some of it, was people were afraid of that dirty, awful outside air that would contaminate the computers," he jokes.

Lawrence Berkeley Lab did a study that showed that with very modest air filtration, the outside air could be cleaner than re-circulated air. The study helped lower the resistance to the idea. Rumsey, Traber and Bulger continually proposed it as they worked on data centers in the Bay Area.

"A lot of our data center work came from knowing that we're in a really great (cool) climate and knowing that computers are a lot more resilient than they used to be," says Bulger. "We'd do a lot of quick upfront analysis to show building owners what the weather looked like in their areas and we were saying, 'Look, it shouldn't be cold in your data center; you should feel comfortable or warm even in most of your facilities.' If we can show that most of these machines run at super

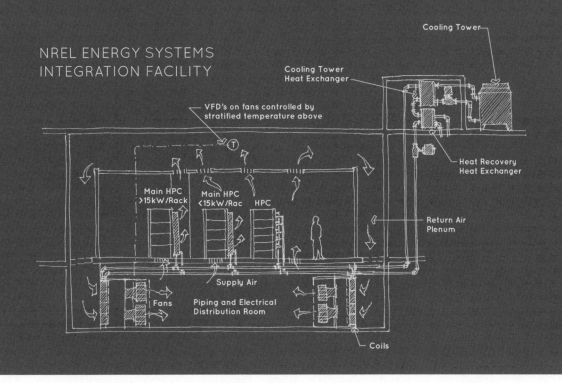

Cooling Tower

Cooling Tower
Heat Exchanger

VFD's on fans controlled by
stratified temperature above

Heat Recovery
Heat Exchanger

Main HPC
>15kW/Rack

Main HPC
<15kW/Rac

HPC

Return Air
Plenum

Supply Air

Fans

Piping and Electrical
Distribution Room

Coils

high temperatures, we can start to have conversations about being able to use outside air economizers 80 percent or more of the year."

As data centers and lab facilities started to take off they became a building type of their own. In typical commercial and residential buildings, energy use is driven by a need to maintain uniform cooling or thermal comfort for people. In data centers, energy use is driven by a process and a need for continuous operation and continuous cooling, mostly for machines that can operate at pretty high temperatures.

As this process-driven building type grew, PG&E and other California utilities were evolving their energy efficiency incentive and rebate programs for their customers. The incentive programs focus on rewarding low energy designs in a one-time cash incentive for each kilowatt-hour saved in the first year of operation. When Bulger and Traber started working with PG&E in 2003, there was no such thing as a defined baseline for high-tech, process-driven facilities, such as data centers or labs or cleanrooms. Working with PG&E, they defined baselines for each of these facility types and published best practice guides to help shape the high-tech incentive programs.

71

"In the early days as data centers were becoming more prevalent and they were realizing that data centers use a lot of energy, we were at the same time designing those data centers in parallel," Bulger explains. Since then, Traber and Bulger have worked with hundreds of data centers on energy efficiency projects, big and small alike.

Bringing in outside air to cool a data center was a radical idea in 2003, but it is more accepted now, especially for a client who has an ambitious energy goal, like National Renewable Energy Lab (NREL). In the recent case of designing the lab's Energy Systems Integration Facility (ESIF), a new super-efficient data center in Golden, CO, when Bulger analyzed the use of outside air, he found it did not actually provide enough energy savings to meet the project goals.

Bulger and his modeling team worked on design energy modeling and did a lot of upfront work studying Golden's climate, looking at how dry it was and understanding the site resources.

Armed with this information and understanding how big the data center was and how much air they could move, they figured out that even with the most efficient fan system they were still shy of the high goals. The air was simply not dense enough and they would have to go with a water-based system that would use less energy to transport heat, perhaps ironic in a high desert. The design recirculates water through the computers and relies solely on evaporation with no refrigerant compressors. (While the team considered water use issues, energy was a higher priority.)

Bulger's team came in early at the concept level and continued on as the analysis arm of the project, so even as the design was getting further along and NREL started to buy certain pieces of equipment or wonder if they could change the size of the pipes on the project, the modeling team would do a calculation against their original calculations and find out if they were going to go over their energy goal.

"We were able to set the foundation with the analysis at the beginning of the project that gave them four or five options of whole different designs and the energy values that each one brings. Then once the client picked their preferred design, we stayed with them, continually informing decisions though the whole process. It was a really great project because they had such ambitious goals," comments Bulger.

Not only is the data center as efficient as the client wanted, NREL is also using the data center's waste heat. "So we got to make a very efficient data center, which is really just a ginormous toaster, and use that free waste heat to heat their building because it gets cold in the winter," Bulger adds.

On ESIF, Bulger's team was able to leverage all the modeling tools they had created for themselves over the years of doing consulting work for PG&E and high-tech clients. "We had created a lot of tools simply to help ourselves do the work. That helped us a lot with our analytical rigor," Bulger says.

Modeling leads to innovative design solutions and modeling itself is innovative, reinventing its own tools and customizing and replicating. Traber and Bulger and their team have built up a set of modular analysis tools, all in a state of evolution.

"For a long time, off-the-shelf modeling software has left something to be desired," comments Traber. "We got frustrated and said, we're not going to accept this poor answer; we're going to pull this software apart and find out what makes it tick and force it to do what we want it to do, or we're just going to build our own model. This sort of tenacity has paid off in the long run."

"Third-party modeling software is evolving rapidly now, and we are changing with it to relearn how to approach design," reflects Bulger. "The way we've done design on our successful projects has worked and they've all been unique. We're now learning to replicate our processes."

They have found that a rough model, "or a 'scrappier' model, to use Kevin's word, is the best model," Bulger says. "So to show the value of a lot of different façade options, our approach is to create just ten models that each hold a little bit of water in terms of looking between them. We shifted a lot to focusing our tools and processes on being faster up front and realizing that ideas are going to change. It requires being very open with people on the team and understanding how the design process can veer all the time. We are starting to use simpler tools like SketchUp and others."

"We are focusing in on the essence of the issue at hand and doing away with any excess baggage, so we are able to iterate through a lot of different combinations rapidly and illustrate the sensitivity in terms of energy use or cost performance," explains Traber. "As you range through some of the

**Sunpath Study and
Shading Analysis**

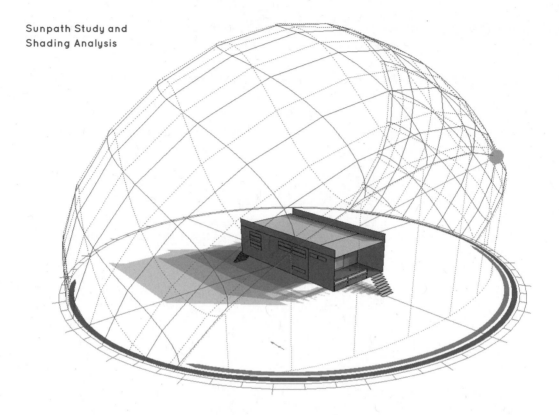

variables, you can show where the sweet spots are. Without having the final precise answer, you can paint a picture."

There's a lot more data now available so instead of being completely in the dark on how much energy the building might use, there are many more benchmarks out there. "We have our own projects, we have our own office for that matter, to see if we are completely off the charts or not," Bulger says.

"In the past we would try to get a lot of detailed information on the programming of the building and we'd tell the owner we really need to know exactly how many people are going to be in the building and where they're going to sit and all these things, and the owner would just look at you with a blank face and say, 'I don't even know how many people work for me now.'"

"So, instead of asking hundreds of questions, I think we are getting smarter. We just ask for the energy bills and a few key questions and limit our input to our models. Instead of having one hundred inputs, we have ten really important ones and we make quality assumptions that get us in the right ballpark for what we're examining—net zero or some other target or just basic performance."

So, this approach has less cost, less stress, and they can help the architects more with fast turn around by asking a small number of pointed questions.

For years, a lot of the modeling team's income came from helping with LEED documentation and CA energy codes. "Now we're using all the skills we learned doing that to create this rapid modeling service that's effective for charrettes and schematic design. And we're getting a new type of business. We're working with developers, using modeling to answer questions like 'can we develop this whole city block?'"

"LEED certification is still going strong, but now there's a lot more buzz around net zero energy buildings and Living Buildings," says Traber. "It gives us new things to think about and new challenges."

Bulger believes these new higher standards that require monitoring are responsible for making everyone on the team, and especially the modelers, more accountable for knowing what they are doing and what they are telling people. "It's making us more honest and we're having higher quality conversations with architects and owners about actual performance and not just theoretical performance," he says.

"With LEED and codes, we made sure our projects performed but it wasn't a requirement of the project. And no one was monitoring it. The first LEED buildings were all over the map in terms of actual performance."

"Now we train our modelers not to quantify performance until we're really sure the building will meet it. If the building doesn't match our predicted performance once it's up and running, we know we will get a call."

"Net zero is very challenging. It's black or white. You either make it or you don't," says Traber.

Another new area of emphasis for the modeling team is around comfort issues. They are currently working with a Silicon Valley tech company on thermal comfort and visual comfort for a new building campus.

"We evaluated, is this design more comfortable than another design? This is intuitive. Anyone sitting within five feet of a glass wall is likely not going to feel comfortable if the sun is shining on that glass wall. You can say that a lot, but after a while it definitely helps to have a thermal model to put a temperature to it," Bulger explains.

The modeling team has created a new section of their services to help put some numbers around these issues. "There's not that many people out there who actually do glare analysis, or daylight analysis," Bulger comments. "That's where I want to expand our team because I think knowing what's visually comfortable and what's thermally comfortable is what is needed in the industry."

We may not need a model to be aware that the sun glinting off our monitor makes it hard to see, or that the giant glass wall near our cube is freezing/burning, but these comfort issues continue to be prevalent in all our work spaces and Bulger hopes models can help address this reality.

Modeling validates what we already sense and Traber says we need to demystify it as a process. "Models should connect people to the physical principles involved and the principles are actually quite simple. You really don't need a lot of math. My desire is to get energy modeling out of the mysterious box. You start talking energy modeling to most people and their eyes glaze over," Traber says. "Can we boil down the important essentials and make them so clear and obvious that more people catch on and it just becomes a part of the culture of design?" he asks.

"All our models are really trying to capture our own common sense or what we feel we understand," explains Bulger. So, models prove that efficient lights are efficient and an efficient envelope is efficient, "and a model is just a way of trying to put a lot of those together and see the synergies, but at the end of the day it should just make practical sense or there should be a good explanation for it. A lot of successful projects are ones that paint a picture that says, 'you know you could have done this without a model.' The old way of modeling evaluated designs after the fact. The valuable shift in modeling practices is that now it validates great ideas before they are drawn."

The User Experience

That an energy modeling team is creating a new division around comfort issues is a reflection of the fact that, more and more, sustainable design is occupant driven. Today, the occupant is the star of high-performance. We cannot hit net zero without influencing tenant decisions and occupant behavior around energy use. We also have office buildings—Google's new campus in Bay View and other new Silicon Valley offices, for example, or Clif Bar's headquarters in Emeryville—that have performance goals completely related to occupant comfort, happiness and productivity.

In 2012, a jury of Berkeley's Center for the Built Environment (CBE) Industry Partners selected the Clif Bar building as one of the winners of the Livable Building Awards. "These projects meet the highest standards for providing healthy and productive indoor environments, and represent best practices for sustainability and overall design," CBE explains.

Clif Bar Headquarters

In some ways, this is the ultimate green building award because the building's own occupants ranked the building's comfort and the award shows the occupants are really happy with their office environment.

The Clif Bar goals were to create a creative space where workers felt happy and productive and collaborative. The design team provided the occupants access to both interactive and private spaces and a lot of opportunities for interaction with plants and nature.

"It's a beautiful building. There are bikes and surfboards hanging from the ceiling," says Bradshaw, who managed the project for Intégral. "But the award has less to do with what Intégral did and more to do with what the architects [ZGF architects] did," he adds. The architecture is impressive. However, Bradshaw's team did contribute to several of the categories that scored high with occupants such as thermal comfort, air quality and acoustics.

Clif Bar goes after the outdoor adventure crowd for the sales of their products, and the people who work there pride themselves on their enthusiasm for outdoor activities and connecting with wilderness and nature. So, above all, the owners and design team wanted the building to reflect the values and culture of the company, which is about being outside.

The 75,000-square-foot LEED Platinum building was originally a World War II valve manufacturing facility. The architects incorporated a bouldering wall, door handles made from bike gears, courtyards, living walls, natural materials, Zen rock gardens and healthy food in an on-site organic café—all design elements and amenities that fit the personality and culture of the Clif Bar worker.

The workspace also offers on-site daycare and provides flexible spaces to accommodate drop-in telecommuters and people who choose alternative work schedules, addressing some of the cultural issues that Matthiessen asserts can attract a more diverse workforce.

The engineering fits in and crosses over into the design. Operable windows provide occupants fresh air, cooling, and connection to the outdoors and more than 90 percent of the occupied space is naturally daylit, according to the award submission.

A large solar array makes the building what Bradshaw calls "grid neutral," meaning it is net zero electricity (not net zero energy). Solar thermal panels heat 70 percent of the building's hot water.

Intégral's David Kaneda did the electrical engineering for the building. To keep the electrical load low, occupancy sensors and timers control the lighting. Task lighting and individual occupancy sensors at each workstation plus daylight sensors also reduce lighting energy use.

One of the areas that scored fairly high with occupants, relative to other projects, was acoustics. "CBE's surveys find that acoustics is the only area where performance is actually getting worse," says Bradshaw. Because they use fewer materials, high-performance building designs often include more hard surfaces in vast open areas, which may look beautiful, but also cause sound to echo and reverberate. Sustainable HVAC systems also tend to be quieter. That can be a nice thing, since a certain part of our brain is constantly working to block out sounds like the hum of an HVAC while we are at work, but quieter systems mean ambient noise, phones and hallway or open area conversations are all the more prevalent.

High-performance design, with its emphasis on using less material, poses a unique challenge for acoustics. Masking sound is important and designing spaces that provide enough private spaces for phone conversations and small meetings is essential.

Clif Bar scored above average on acoustics, perhaps in part because the design includes a lot of break out areas where small meetings and discussions can take place out of earshot of those working in open areas. ZGF architect Kathy Berg adds, "We installed recycled blue jean material and PEPP panels (Porous Expanded Polypropylene) in the ceiling to reduce reflected noise. Low workstations that provide visual access to nearby employees allow staff to modulate their voices so they don't disturb coworkers. (Low stations work better than high cubes despite the extra absorptive materials.) Workstations are grouped with typically six and no more than eight people and include acoustic tack panels."

Sound and, more importantly, quiet are valuable areas for improvement for the performance of buildings and health and well-being of people in the future.

Engineering for Health

Healthy buildings are important for office workers, but places of healing also need to provide clean fresh air and a quality and comfortable indoor environment.

When you walk by old hospital buildings in places like New York City, you often see these big screened-in porches that overlook lawns and trees where patients convalesced. Fresh air was once prescribed as medicine itself, especially for TB patients. But most of these beautiful hospitals are closed or repurposed and if you go and visit someone in a modern hospital, you are not likely to feel any breezes and you are somewhat susceptible to get sick yourself.

"The hospital of the future is really just the hospital of the past," says Hydes, who spent much of his career working on healthcare facilities. "Hospitals 100 years ago were designed so that every patient had an operable window, so they were naturally ventilated and they were always on the top of the biggest hill so they got wind (fresh air). San Francisco's Laguna Honda is a great example," he says. "In almost every major city you'll find the hospitals on the high point."

According to what Hydes calls 'his version of history', modern healthcare began with the Victorians, who used to put all patients in one big room. At some point they started putting people in private rooms and they got rid of natural ventilation and started using mechanical ventilation. Everything was going just fine until the late 60s and 70s when we started to air condition hospitals. They were still bringing outside air in until the 70s oil crisis and then the standards changed, according to Hydes. "Because of the oil crisis, they started to recirculate two-thirds of the air. You now have your private room but you're breathing re-circulated air, which is why, if you want to get sick, go to a hospital."

In fact, recirculating air in hospitals helps spread airborne infections, viruses, germs and bacteria. "Only now, two or three decades later, finally, people are realizing this is a problem and we are re-writing the standards," says Hydes.

Laguna Honda Hospital, 1959

"Fast forward to the hospital of the future. And now, we get on a plane and we go to Europe and specifically to Sweden and we find the greenest hospitals in the world, and they are all doing exactly what we did back 100 years ago, but more efficiently with better glass and better walls."

"In the States, they don't often naturally ventilate healthcare buildings," comments Doug Kerr of Elementa, Intégral Group's London office. "They just seal the building up and put lots of heating and cooling in. In the United States the worry is if you open a window you'll let in every bug and disease."

Every bug and disease is often aided in travel by the mechanical system when indoor air is recirculated in hospitals. The alternative might be to filter this air, but if opening windows on the perimeter is just as healthy and saves tons of energy and lowers emissions, filtering for all rooms seems senseless.

"What we've been doing over here in the United Kingdom for some time now is working very hard to naturally ventilate buildings, and we only put in mechanical vents and/or cooling where specific clinical needs drive it."

So, they wouldn't naturally ventilate an operating room but, Kerr says, a consulting and examination room is "basically an office with a wash-hand basin." For deep areas, they put in fresh air mechanical ventilation with a little bit of filtration, but not high levels, and they won't recirculate air. High grade HEPA filtration goes only in operating rooms and clinical areas. "We work from the premise of what can we not put in," explains Kerr.

Brierley Hill Health Centre

Brierley Hill hospital is a 20 million pound sterling health facility in the Midlands. It is a brand new building on a large intersection with a major primary arterial road going down one side of it. It's an example of how working the latitude within regulations that are designed to protect people's health actually resulted in a healthier building than would have been built if they followed the regulations without questioning them. The success of the building required everyone from the architect to the occupant to change and approach the building completely differently in order to make fresh air a priority.

Basically, Kerr's team asked the architect to completely replan the building as a result of the location of the road. "What we managed to do was get the non-clinical functions on the side away from the road, and that meant we could rely on natural ventilation," Kerr explains.

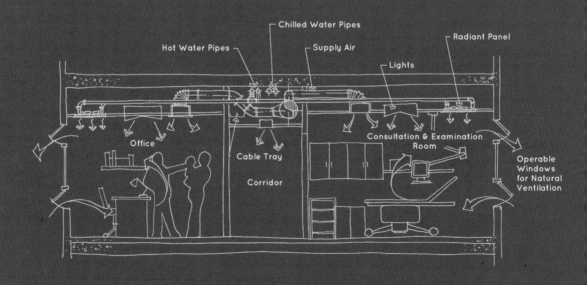

BRIERLEY HILL HEALTH CENTRE

If they would have put any of these patient rooms on the other side, the noise and the fumes would have been intrusive and unacceptable. They moved all the rooms that needed clinical ventilation on to the side next to the road, and they simply do not open the windows on that side.

The stakeholders, the users, were a little bit concerned, Kerr says, because they were used to having the adjacencies a certain way. They had to change the way they work a little bit. "We worked with them to really look at the building services within the building to say, what can we do to reduce the reliance on mechanical systems and what can we do to maximize natural ventilation. Not everybody will buy into accepting different ways of working, but those enlightened ones bought into it," says Kerr. These are the kinds of exceptional clients Hydes refers to earlier.

In the United Kingdom they have Health Technical Memorandums (HTM), which provide requirements from the Department of Health for healthcare institutional design, Kerr explains. "The problem with HTMs is they are far too generic, so the same HTM applies for natural ventilation whether it's a small hospital, a doctor's practice, or a big acute trauma center," says Kerr. "So we challenged that."

At Brierley Hill, 40 percent of the building is not medical in its true sense. There are offices, meeting rooms, and staff rooms. "So why apply the HTM that invariably required more complexity?" asks Kerr. "Why don't we treat that 40 percent of the building like a commercial office, because that's what it is?"

Kerr's team made a case to the Primary Care Trust. They complied with the HTM in all medical areas, but treated the rest like a commercial space. "They went along with that because it was a significant cost savings to the Primary Care Trust," says Kerr. "That was the real driver, to be perfectly honest, not sustainability."

This solution saved everyone money because the hospital was financed with private sector funding. In this Public-Private-Partnership (PPP) arrangement, the developer owns and maintains the facility. "The developer was very keen to keep costs down," say Kerr. "We managed to provide an incredibly energy-efficient and healthy building without a huge amount of renewable technologies. It was about the thermal efficiency of the building, and the quality of the glazing." (The majority of the heating is ceiling mounted radiant panels.)

Performance Engineering

Performance comes from design and it comes from operation. Buildings of all types often do not perform as they were intended to. Hospitals, labs, commercial offices, university buildings—all these building types often need major and minor ongoing adjustments after occupancy.

James Goodall, principal of Intégral's Calgary office, went around and examined healthcare facilities in North America after they were operating and found a 97.3 percent failure rate, meaning almost 100 percent of the time the buildings were not operating as intended. And after making modifications (after commissioning) the failure rate was still greater than 66 percent.

Goodall happened to look at healthcare facilities in this case, but he has found similar failure rates and dysfunction in office buildings. During one emergency simulation, "the building didn't detect there was a fire. The exhaust systems didn't exhaust smoke. The stairwell and security access was locking people in the stairwell," says Goodall.

Goodall often draws on his performance commissioning experience working with military, government and private organizations where he was involved with developing quality control and testing practices for all kinds of technologies from submarines to airplanes to oil refineries, and he asks: "Would you get in an aircraft and fly away knowing that it had a 97.3 percent initial failure rate?"

It is amazing that we have this expanding movement with greater and greater numbers of low energy, net zero and Living Buildings, but if you go in and test any recently completed buildings after it's occupied you very often will find it is not operating as it was intended, observes SK Lai, managing principal in Intégral's Vancouver office. "This makes people cynical or defensive, depending on which side of the building design you are on."

Designing is only part of creating and sustaining high-performance buildings. "Our analysis and research shows that where we need to focus most in all building types is in the occupancy and the ongoing operations and maintenance of these facilities," says Goodall, who has spent a lot of his career trying to get clients to do what he calls "real commissioning."

Commissioning—checking the performance of the building against the owner's requirements and intentions and then making modifications to optimize it once it is operating—has been a crucial aspect of sustainable design that separates it from traditional design where it is, unfortunately, absent.

As high-performance buildings took hold, building owners and designers began to understand the importance of creating an appropriate commissioning program for the building. The arrival of LEED and a burgeoning interest in ensuring performance really created a place for commissioning. However, teams still tend to walk away from the building at occupancy. Not only does commissioning need to be a widespread and common practice, but it needs to be recurring and more comprehensive to really optimize performance. Goodall has a few ideas about that.

Commissioning is a quality control process with documented confirmation that building systems are planned, designed, installed, tested, operated and maintained in compliance with the owner's project requirement and design intent.

In addition to verifying the building's performance before it is occupied, commissioning agents set up a program for building owners for ongoing support and continuous optimization of the building. A well-rounded commissioning program will enable the owner to carry out renovations and modifications to the building and complete the necessary fine-tuning adjustments that optimize the building over the entire life cycle.

Now that commissioning is somewhat more prevalent, at least in sustainable design, even more comprehensive service offerings have begun to arise within the industry—re-commissioning, retro-commissioning, continuous commissioning —all facets of commissioning a building that attempt to address this need for continuing to pay attention to, test and adjust buildings over the long run. Goodall has used his experience in the healthcare sector to take the idea of commissioning further by developing a concept called "performance engineering," or PxEng.

"Commissioning is only one facet of performance engineering," he says. "During commissioning, systems are usually tested individually. Very seldom, if ever, was there the ability to tie them together and find out how these systems interact and communicate. No one was testing these as a whole."

PxEng integrates testing and the interaction of multiple systems at the whole building level. All available information pertaining to the operation, maintenance and trouble shooting of the building is also digitized, creating a cradle to now history or "pedigree" for the building. Immediately accessible to authorized personnel, regardless of their geographic location, people involved in the maintenance of the building keep up and use the pedigree throughout the life of the building to organize and find information on the building. The pedigree makes available information such as system design intent, operational performance, preventative maintenance schedules and records, and as-built drawings.

A number of facilities have successfully integrated PxEng into the building life cycle. One large-scale healthcare facility—an immense, complex facility with a construction budget of more than $1.5 billion—asked Goodall and his team to come in a third of the way through construction to implement a standard commissioning process.

The facility has operating rooms, neo-natal, ultra clean rooms—every service you can imagine within a healthcare environment. "This is an incredibly sophisticated facility. These environments are extremely delicate and all these systems have to work in tandem with each other," says Goodall.

Working with people within the facility, his team lobbied the owners, healthcare groups, anyone who would listen, to give them a chance to implement integration testing on the facility. The stakes were just high enough in this incredibly complex healthcare facility that the commissioning team was able to convince the design team to carry out what Goodall says is probably the largest integration test ever undertaken in healthcare. "In a lot of instances, the operators never see the building lose power and they don't know what to do when it does happen," he says. They were able to test for that and every failure concept they could come up with.

"People swore up and down that this facility was ready to go. However, when we conducted our initial testing, we identified significant failures," Goodall says. After

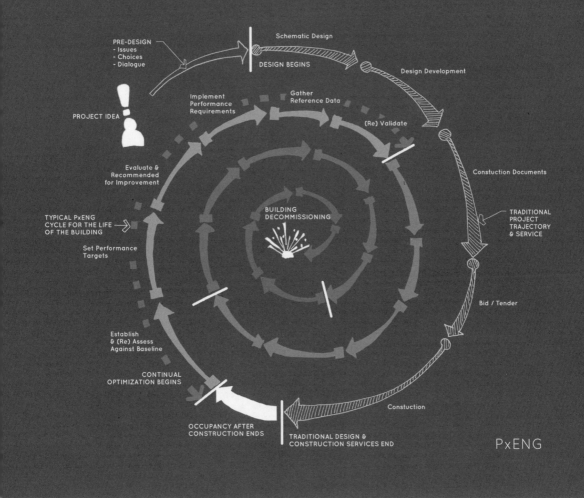

PxENG

the initial integration testing, hundreds and hundreds of minor modifications were made to programming, design, logic and process. Primarily they made changes to the software, integration of the health and safety operations and how they communicate and interact. They also tweaked emergency power systems and how they come on and how they operate. They repeatedly tested for whether there was continuity and dependability.

"It is now performing far and away closer to the original design than it would have without the integration testing," says Goodall.

In the course of creating the integration testing, Goodall's team also created customized QR codes for each piece of equipment and documented all the information pertaining to each piece of equipment within the pedigree.

The buildings industry in North America was paper-based until recently. No databases, no audio capture, no video capture, no laser scanning. "Now, you can scan the QR Code on a piece of equipment, a pump for example, with your iPad and immediately find out who sold us that pump, who tested it, how it performed, is there a maintenance program, and all this information," Goodall says.

To show how helpful the digital approach can be in an emergency situation, he points to a test he did while commissioning a commercial office tower. The design team conducted a test of the smoke control systems within the building, looking to verify that the HVAC systems would in fact remove the smoke from the facility and enable occupant evacuation. Everything sequenced as intended, except the smoke evacuation fans turned off instead of on, and the entire facility was actually filling with smoke. They had hundreds of workers who were unable to move in the facility because of thick smoke and the whole facility was in fire mode.

The building operator was able to scan the QR code of the equipment and instantly had access to the emergency procedures for bypassing the automatic mode for the smoke control system, enabling manual control. "The individuals didn't have to go down to the control room, look through books, get drawings. They were able to activate the smoke control fans manually and exhaust the smoke right there," Goodall explains.

Being able to act quickly is part of PxEng. It's also exactly what the operations and maintenance people need to help maintain the building well over its life. Goodall hopes it becomes standard practice and not an add-on with additional costs. "You used to have to pay a premium to get an AutoCAD drawing. Everything was done by hand and if you wanted a digital drawing it was a big deal. Well now that's common. You expect digital drawings. I'd like PxEng to find its way to that level," he says.

"When you allow the building to run in an optimal way, you are actually using fewer resources, spending less money on the building," adds Lai. "You actually are operating at net zero instead of just intending to."

"Having all the information digitized and in one single location allows you to move in time alongside the building. It allows this life cycle picture to develop so you can actually see the entire picture of how it got started to the day you want to decommission it," explains Lai.

This allows learning from buildings. The digital pedigree assists the building engineer in conducting a proper analysis when a system is not performing as intended. Once the issue is resolved, the engineer can update and enhance the information with additional details and lessons learned.

Using what they learn from buildings, engineers can create rule sets to guide the building operation," says Lai. "As more rule sets are developed, artificial intelligence will begin."

While it's easy to see why this kind of documenting and testing is extremely helpful for complex buildings like hospitals, design firms are applying it to all kinds of projects. For example, buildings that are pursuing the International Living Future Institute's Living Building or Net Zero Certification, like the Simon Fraser UniverCity (SFU) Childcare in Vancouver, are using PxEng as part of the monitoring process that is required for the full year after occupancy.

Living Buildings like SFU's UniverCity Childcare Centre really promote this idea of transparency of energy use and of materials, with monitoring requirements, Red Lists for materials and requirements to disclose ingredients in building products so we know they meet standards of health. Transparency is a key factor leading to higher performance in buildings.

"Revealing information creates its own behavior changes and literal changes in performance," says McLennan. "People not only need to monitor their buildings in terms of how they perform, they actually need to communicate that to users and buyers."

This post-design phase, testing, monitoring, optimizing, working with occupants on plug loads, is becoming a bigger part of the work of sustainable design and engineering firms. Toronto Principal Chris Piche, who works on PxEng with Goodall, says the post-occupancy phase is as critical to the success of the building as the design phase. "Building life cycle means that you have a client for life. As an integrated design firm, we want to work alongside our clients as partners focused on the successful operation of the building—for life."

Occupants and Performance

The David and Lucile Packard Foundation building, a net zero energy building in Los Altos, CA, recently asked Intégral and the post-occupancy team to stay on after the first year of occupancy to eighteen months for further optimization. "They still see value in us staying on. We've done this on our own before. It's an interesting relationship to develop with a building owner. It's about the relationship and the people. They are so satisfied with the building they don't want to let us go. It's a lot of fun for us," says Principal Eric Soladay.

Just as in the PxEng concept and approach, the post-occupancy team has a very robust control systems and monitoring systems for Packard. They're doing minute-by-minute data. They have every circuit on the building monitored. The entire post-occupancy team gets the building alarms emailed to them. "We're right there with them. We're not just handing it over and saying, you guys operate it now. We're able to address problems in real time," says Soladay.

As designs get greener, the plug load is playing a more important role. Occupant behavior is one of the most important influences on energy savings. Packard's commitment to energy savings in their equipment choices reduced the plug loads by 58 percent. Packard also commissioned Intégral to do a detailed study of building plug use and, as a result of information in the study, the occupants are now responsible for something more like an 80 percent plug load reduction.

"There has always been this attitude of I can't control plug loads. I can't help it if someone brings in a microwave," David Kaneda says. "Now, as soon as you say net zero, you better look at plug loads. It went from this thing no one paid any attention to, to a necessary part of reaching net zero."

"The first time Peter [Rumsey] and I worked on it was my office [the IDeAs net zero office] because I had control over the plug loads," Kaneda recalls. "It was mostly just swapping out flat screens and installing occupancy sensors and using

Plug Load Reduction Study

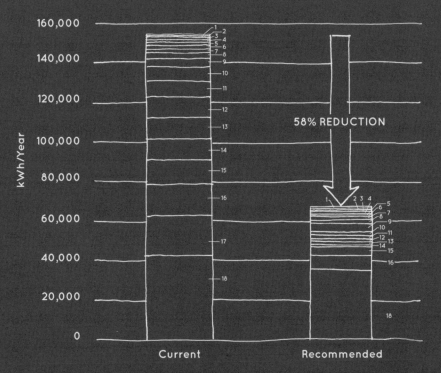

PACKARD PLUG LOAD REDUCTION STUDY

Energy Star equipment. But even if it's Energy Star and you leave it in standby, it's using a lot of energy. You have to turn it off. But if you turn printers off, it takes them awhile to warm up once you turn them back on. They're not ready on demand."

For reducing plug loads, appropriate controls on efficient equipment is the key, according to Kaneda. "There are three ways to control it," he says: Occupancy sensors; software to power it down (as in sleep controls on your laptop); and time-based controls.

"Time-based controls can do things like power down your cable box at night in a residence. The cable box is a huge energy suck and runs all the time so it doesn't have to go through a delay to download the cable information whenever you want to turn it on," Kaneda explains. Chances are you won't need to turn it on at 3 a.m. very often, so a timer turning it down during the night could save you a lot energy.

Another idea for commercial buildings is to use your security system to time turn off of printers and other equipment, Kaneda advises. If the last person is leaving and turns on the alarm, no one will need the printer until the first person arrives and turns off the alarm.

Dashboards, like those in the Packard building and in the living room of Kaneda's net zero Cupertino home, are also becoming more prevalent in helping with transparency. "If people have this information about their energy use, they will adjust their behavior," Kaneda says, noting that he can see when his children are watching television by looking at his home's dashboard on his laptop.

According to Soladay, this is definitely where buildings are going: simple, easy to use devices with a tremendous amount of brains behind them. But dashboards and apps have to provide the right information for the user. The facilities guy needs different information than the tenant who just wants to know what his cubicle is doing.

"These kinds of things are important. They don't save energy by themselves," says Kaneda. "Some of it is the building. But the building itself doesn't solve the problem. People do."

Through analysis and transparency, through building controls, through monitoring, we can create this loop of learning from buildings and see their performance increase over their lives. We are creating an intelligent synergy between the building and the occupant. Performance comes in thinking of buildings and their occupants as living organisms that can grow, learn and perform better over time.

"WE ARE CREATING AN INTELLIGENT SYNERGY BETWEEN THE BUILDING AND THE OCCUPANT. PERFORMANCE COMES IN THINKING OF BUILDINGS AND THEIR OCCUPANTS AS LIVING ORGANISMS THAT CAN GROW, LEARN AND PERFORM BETTER OVER TIME."

ACCELERATE

94

VanDusen Botanical Garden Visitor Center

O3

The actual value of some things exceeds human ability to calculate or measure...

— Wendell Berry, 2012 Jefferson Lecture

Accelerate

Imagine a child who spends every single school day in a building like Clearview Elementary School in Hanover, PA, Fossil Creek High School in Fort Collins, CO, or the Bertschi School in Seattle, a Living Building. She and her classmates simply learn more and retain knowledge better as a direct result of better air and natural light in their schools. She may be exposed to rainwater collection and PV panels and daily see how these systems conserve resources and reduce pollution and greenhouse gas emissions. She might be in a class designed to function around the school's energy and water systems. Her school may recycle and compost and teach the idea that there is no "away." This building changes her health, her education and expectations and, perhaps, her character.

Thanks to a green school movement promoted by the U.S. Green Building Council, the Collaborative for High Performance Schools and others, millions of students have attended thousands of LEED-certified schools. And when these students graduate from high school and seek higher education, chances are very high that they will find themselves at a university with a sustainability directive and green buildings on campus.

As students come out of school and begin their professional lives, they are facing greater and greater challenges to health, environment and economic well-being, and our only hope is that they are aware and prepared. A huge number of influences may shape their values around health and sustainability, and green buildings are part of that influence.

No amount of green building evangelism has been as effective for the acceleration of green design as the growing number of green buildings where we can spend time. The buildings themselves teach and influence all of us who pass through them, and we can be very deliberate about making these buildings teaching tools to promote awareness around systems and design elements.

"The buildings themselves teach and influence all of us who pass through them, and we can be very deliberate about making these buildings teaching tools to promote awareness around systems and design elements."

The unique rainwater catchment system, a centerpiece of the design in the LEED Platinum Natural Science building at Mills College, provides a beautiful example of how to teach and inspire occupants, students and visitors, not through the placards and dashboards LEED typically gives education points for, but through integration with art. Since the building was completed in 2007, a courtyard display of the system has been showing how catchment works and quietly revealing the preciousness and beauty of the cycles of rain affecting our natural and built environment.

As visitors come into the lobby of the science building, they look out into a courtyard and see the catchment system. When it is raining, rainwater pours from the downspout on the roof and flows into a series of metal pans shaped like lily pads, finally cascading down into the stainless steel holding tank, a recycled mayonnaise container.

"The idea was, when it's raining you see this sculpture come alive and this water cascading down. And when it's not raining, you just see the sculpture, but it's quiet, it's dormant, and so you get a connection to the rainwater and to the seasonality of nature," says Rumsey who helped design the system along with Intégral Principal Susan Ecker and in collaboration with the school, the rest of the design team, and local artist Archie Held.

The 2000-gallon stainless steel mayonnaise container collects up to 60,000 gallons of water a year for flushing toilets, according to Mills.

The gear that takes the rainwater and filters it, puts it through a UV light, pumps it and sends it off to the toilets, is visible in the lobby, in a softly lit closet covered by a screen mesh. A diagram shows passersby how the system works.

"We did another building on the same campus (the graduate school of business) where the system ended up buried in a crawl space," Ecker recalls. This is the more typical application, and that system works really well, but the catchment system as art has other ongoing positive effects. For example, the Port of San Francisco pulled out slides of the cascading Mills system when they discussed stormwater solutions for the Bay Area. Furthermore, photos of the Mills

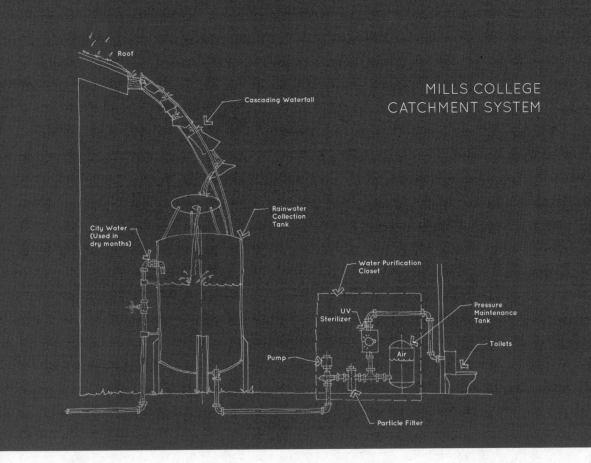

College system show up in slideshows and articles all the time, teaching and demonstrating the benefits of capturing rainwater while subtly reinforcing the notion of the valuable nature and life-giving beauty of water.

In addition to the water features, the Mills Science building incorporates energy-efficient glass and daylighting, occupancy sensors, and photovoltaic panels on the roof provide 30 percent of the building's electricity.

Originally, the Platinum Mills Natural Science building was slated for LEED Silver. The architect, EHDD, proposed waterless urinals to get extra LEED points that would take the building to LEED Gold. (In the end, the client preferred using 0.125 (pint) gallon-per-flush urinals that first came on the market when the project was in construction, Ecker clarifies.)

"The donors pushed for the building to go beyond Gold to Platinum because they knew it would be a better building," Rumsey says. This is acceleration, when the people who are paying for the building advocate for it to be better and greener.

Once people begin a process of participating in innovation they become motivated to push even further as they see a path of positive benefits unfolding.

Lots of schools, university buildings, government buildings and museums (like the Exploratorium in Chapter One, which has a glass mechanical room that shows its unique bay water cooling system) and public buildings serve as demonstrations, constantly influencing the public. These buildings also help design teams, who can point to these systems as examples for reluctant building owners, ESCOs, and developers. It is hard to promote something that you haven't experienced and experiential learning and exposure to positive examples is fundamental to the idea of accelerating change. The success of early LEED Platinum government buildings, such as StopWaste.org's office in Oakland, completed in 2005, are the reason some municipalities now feel they can require LEED standards for government offices.

StopWaste.org is the Alameda County Waste Management Authority and the Alameda County Source Reduction and Recycling Board. Alameda County built the

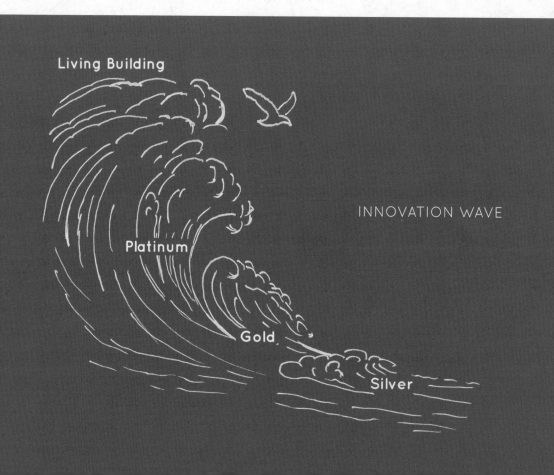

Living Building

INNOVATION WAVE

Platinum

Gold

Silver

StopWaste.org office as one of the first Platinum buildings and the first building to incorporate waterless urinals in Oakland, and they did it on a tight budget.

StopWaste.org, and buildings like it have been a basic catalyst for this acceleration of green design in publicly funded buildings. "This one's simple and affordable. In terms of changing the industry, these are the buildings that make it seem possible," says Bradshaw, who was the project manager on this, his first LEED Platinum building.

StopWaste.org provided a compelling model for going further without costing more. The building owners were at first going for LEED Silver when they approached staff at Intégral. Bradshaw explains, "We did modeling to determine how much insulation was necessary to avoid mechanical systems." Trading out mechanical costs for a better envelope was the trigger point that allowed them to go for LEED Platinum without adding extra costs. (The building has 18-inch-thick, R60 insulation.) By working together to take the building further than its original goal, the design team and the building owners created a viable example Intégral staff could point to as they worked to push other buildings further.

The insulation is invisible to the public, but StopWaste.org gives educational tours to show off the building's PV system, water-saving urinals, energy-efficient windows, energy-efficient lighting and daylight harvesting systems. Members of the public frequent the building, seeing and using its high-performance systems, while attending public hearings in its boardrooms and working with StopWaste.org staff on community initiatives. In this way, by touching and seeing these systems, people have quietly come to expect certain green features that conserve water and energy in public buildings.

There are many public demonstration buildings like the StopWaste.org building now and they have been triggers for more. Acceleration has happened. The edge has moved.

Now, demonstration is happening on a much larger scale, literally, in hundreds of thousands of square feet, in buildings like the Infosys Software Development Building (in hot and humid Hyderabad, India), a unique 250,000- square-foot-test case for radiant cooling. The building is split into two symmetric halves, with one half cooled by conventional air conditioning and the other half by radiant cooling. The success of the demonstration project has contributed to the acceleration of millions of square feet of energy-efficient design and radiant cooling, not only in India, but in other places with a similar mindset, such as Silicon Valley.

Acceleration in India

The Infosys demonstration project emerged out of a strange combination of a vision and desire for the most energy-efficient building in the world combined with an entrenched system based in a fear of doing things differently.

"Radiant cooling is accelerating faster in India now, in a more challenging climate, than in the United States. So, this is really a transformative project on a massive scale," says Rumsey, going on to explain how the Infosys building got split in two. The story reveals some typical barriers to implementing innovative systems such as radiant cooling.

Then chairman of Infosys, N.R. Narayana Murthy, co-chaired the World Economic Forum in Davos, Switzerland, in 2005 where discussions on energy and sustainability strongly motivated him to change building practices on the Infosys campus. Through connections at Stanford, where Rumsey teaches classes on buildings systems, Murthy found and contacted Rumsey, and promptly said: "I want you to help design the most energy-efficient building in the world."

Rumsey went to India and spent some time teaching energy-efficient design—good orientation, daylighting, sun shading, efficient cooling systems, and plug loads. The Infosys building was going forward at a good pace. Rumsey went back to Oakland and started doing energy modeling for the building. "Then I started getting these emails questioning the idea of cooling a building with radiant cooling," Rumsey says. "The momentum of the entrenched buildings professionals who had been doing buildings for them for the last twenty years stopped it [the radiant cooling]."

To break the impasse, the construction manager said, "Here's what we're going to do. We're literally going to cut the building in half. On one half we are going to do the best building our local engineers can do and then on the other half we're going to do what Peter tells us to do," recalls Rumsey.

"At first I was really disappointed," says Rumsey. "Then I realized it would be a great opportunity to have a side-by-side comparison of these two systems."

But the obstacles to installing the radiant system did not stop there. Infosys started by building a small sample building, a 2,000 square-foot security building, for the radiant cooling. They didn't have the proper pieces and it didn't work that well. There was water on the floor, for example. "We spent a lot of time convincing them we could do it in the bigger building. The local engineer refused to do the construction drawings on the radiant because they were just not comfortable with it. So we did the detailed construction drawings ourselves," Rumsey recalls.

Eventually the radiant system went in on half of the 250,000-square foot building and worked well. No water on the floor. Infosys put a lot of metering in to compare the traditional Variable Air Volume (VAV) to the radiant system—meters for chilled water flows and airflows and temperature sensors, so they could really understand what was going on in the building. Then they filled the building with 4000-5000 people.

Both sides had the same lighting, the same efficient envelope and the same daylighting, just different mechanical systems, so the VAV system side and the radiant side were done equally in a way that was as efficient as possible.

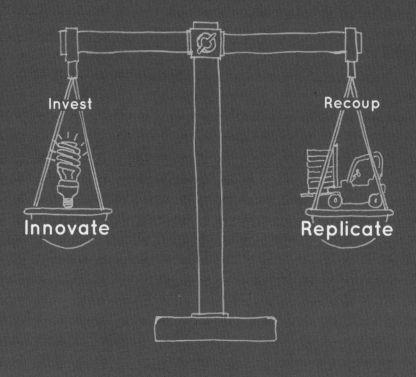

Invest

Recoup

Innovate

Replicate

"The criteria they used for the building is beautifully simple: We will have 100 percent daylight so that in the middle of the day we can turn off all the lights with no direct sun adding to cooling the load," explains Rumsey. They had to develop a sunshade and light shelf system that bounced light into the space with no direct sun. The VAV system also had the advantage of that system. So the cooling load was already 70-80 percent lower for both sides than for other not-so-efficient buildings on the Infosys campus.

When the data from the metering came in, the radiant side performed 35 percent better than the VAV system. Infosys modified an inefficient dehumidification unit and the savings on the radiant side went up to

40 percent. "The real clincher was that the contractor tracked the HVAC system costs. The radiant side cost 9-10 percent less, for materials and labor, than the VAV side. It was cheaper to build and it saved 40 percent of the energy. That's a big win," says Rumsey.

The radiant side not only has lower energy use and lower costs, but the employees are requesting to work on the radiant side due to better comfort. Lower first costs, lower operating costs and better comfort—an ideal solution. After about two years of collecting data, and vetting the system in all seasons, Infosys, convinced of the superiority of radiant cooling, began installing it everywhere. They were building a new building a month all over India. "Now, they are designing all the new company buildings with radiant cooling or chilled beam. They prefer the radiant system. They have several 500,000-square-foot buildings with the radiant," explains Rumsey. This is acceleration.

Intégral is still working with Infosys and working with another client in New Delhi who is building one million square feet of corporate lease space that is going to be radiant as well.

"They are accelerating and leap frogging in India because two-thirds of the buildings they need by 2050 have not yet been built. They are learning quickly and they are not afraid to make mistakes," says Rumsey.

"In India they are reinventing everything now including buildings. Right now there's a culture of innovation and wanting to get out front. It's an excitement for trying new things," he adds. "We take it much more cautiously here in the United States. We do have a culture of innovation here in the United States, but a lot of that is channeled toward things like software and the Internet."

A lot of the buildings they are creating in India will not last more than twenty years. But at Infosys they are also now constructing buildings to last.

"A parallel is Silicon Valley," says Rumsey. "They have said, 'just build me a shell to get going in.'" We are tearing down and retrofitting buildings in Silicon Valley and India that were thrown together really quickly in the last two decades.

Empire State Building as a Model

"When our clients from India came over, they wanted to see the Empire State Building," says Intégral Associate Principal John Weale. They were interested in the possibilities for retrofitting existing buildings the Empire State Building (ESB) showcases.

Weale was involved from the early stages of design and assisted with the energy modeling for the ESB retrofit. From the modeling, the design team made the recommendations to remove the building's sashes and glass from 6,514 windows to clean the panes, and add a low emissivity (low-E) film and gas mixture between the reused panes, creating high-performance, triple-element windows without wasting the existing, relatively new, windows.

Such dramatic improvements to the building envelope as this, and seven other major efficiency measures, were justified by downsizing and eliminating a chiller, rather than the usual practice of replacing and upsizing. This approach saved considerable capital and operating costs, giving the building a three-year payback on its investments in energy efficiency.

The retrofit continues to be widely touted in the media as a template for other sustainable, multi-tenant, multi-story retrofits. It certainly has been successful in terms of drawing bigger, higher-class (literally, Class A) tenants. "People are now renting three or four floors," Weale says. "This is the more profitable tenant they wanted."

As a model for other retrofits, the building is difficult to replicate exactly, Weale says. "There are only a few buildings like this and the chances that they would be undergoing an overall capital improvement project that offers this opportunity is rare."

Weale does view the ESB as a prototype, "but what I have found interesting is that it is a prototype for many different types of projects," he says. "With ESB we did everything and it was a pilot. It was the first of its kind and because of

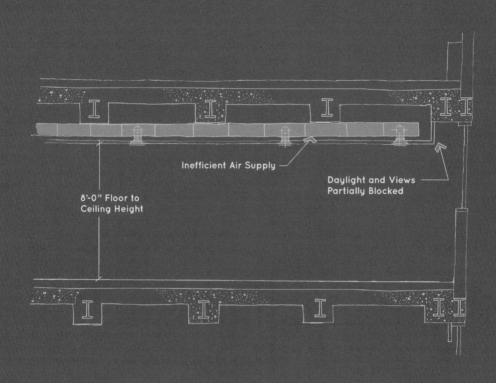

Inefficient Air Supply

Daylight and Views
Partially Blocked

8'-0" Floor to
Ceiling Height

EMPIRE STATE BUILDING – BEFORE

the scale of it and its ambition to pilot a profitable, sustainable retrofit, it was a lot of work and so an exact carbon copy of that process wouldn't really be feasible for very many buildings."

The very first iPhone is not in use anymore and there's a reason for that, Weale says. "The Empire State Building is not something where I would say: here is the exact map. It's more like the ESB provided a toolkit that people can take and put together their own process using those pieces."

Acceleration in this case comes not through direct replication but through adaptation and through applying a similar methodology, though perhaps to different types of projects with different goals and budgets. This retrofit and its accompanying publicity helped validate the design methodology that Intégral, and places like RMI [who, along with JCI, led the project design team],

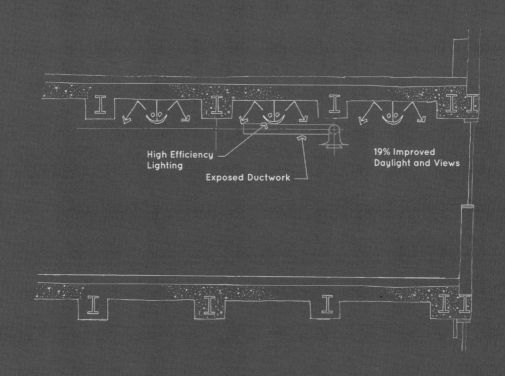

High Efficiency
Lighting

Exposed Ductwork

19% Improved
Daylight and Views

EMPIRE STATE BUILDING – AFTER

have always espoused, says Weale. "The same methodology of bringing the stakeholders together and assessing the demands and the loads first and pushing on imagined boundaries should be used on every project," he says. (Thinking that because ESB was a historic building we can't change the windows was an imagined boundary.)

"Everything I've done since the ESB has been on a smaller budget but has been achieving good results using tools proven at ESB," says Weale.

For example, the National Resources Defense Council (NRDC) is doing a tenant fit out pilot program in New York City that replicates key features of the ESB retrofit, but on a much smaller scale that fits the lower budget available for tenant spaces ranging from 30,000 square feet up to 120,000 square feet.

The ESB design team put together tenant guidelines and requirements for leasing that push efficiency at the tenant level. "Companies are taking 2-4 floors of the ESB and they are trying to apply the Empire State model of doing energy

"THE SAME METHODOLOGY OF BRINGING THE STAKEHOLDERS TOGETHER AND ASSESSING THE DEMANDS AND THE LOADS FIRST AND PUSHING ON IMAGINED BOUNDARIES SHOULD BE USED ON EVERY PROJECT."

modeling, having an energy charrettte, identifying measures, analyzing them with energy modeling, and then hopefully implementing them and finally doing a measurement and verification to confirm they got the savings," explains Weale.

"We've participated in this program for two, going on three tenants of the ESB," says Weale. Intégral has been working with the NRDC's Center for Market Innovation to develop a replicable methodology for tenant fit outs to push valuable pieces of the ESB approach into the lower budget and size fit out market. Intégral is doing the energy modeling on those fit outs and provides the charrette and design recommendations and guidance. Measurement and verification is a key part of the program to provide solid case studies to help encourage adoption of this efficient approach. The pilot program is very popular and there is currently a waiting list.

True Replicability

"It's not the Empire State Building," Gerry Faubert says of a net zero retail bank prototype Intégral's Toronto office is working on.

It may not be a very sexy or iconic project, but in terms of true replicability and acceleration, this modest 6,000-square-foot, net zero prototype is going to traverse Canada in a way that has wide-reaching effects on energy savings and carbon emission reductions. The project has five goals: LEED Gold or Platinum; net zero energy; affordability; scalability and replicability in diverse climates; and constructability.

The highly customizable branch prototype is essentially a kit of parts that will be adapted to different climates throughout Canada. (There are seven diverse climate types across Canada and there may be fifty banks based on this prototype to start. There are more than 1,000 retail branches in Canada for this corporation, which has asked Intégral not to name it at this time.)

The bank branch brings up some somewhat typical challenges for net zero projects on a budget. Because it is net zero, the photovoltaic panels on the roof create all the energy or equivalent that is going to be used in the building. But since the roof space limits the electrical output available from the PV panels, "We had to research the market and find extremely efficient panels, and there's a cost impact. So the challenge is how to be net zero on budget," says the project manager, Salil Ranadive.

The plug loads in the bank are largely responsible for the challenge. Plug loads are a massive amount of what design teams have to worry about on any net zero building, but banks have particularly high equipment needs. "What we discovered is more than 53 percent of energy demand in the building is equipment," says Faubert.

It turns out, coin counters use gobs of electricity. The automatic banking machine cannot completely power down due to security and 24-hour service. In Toronto, and other cold climates, in winter, ATMs need internal heaters to keep their circuit boards from failing. And due to security concerns, the bank is not comfortable with Cloud storage for electronic data at this time, so on-site servers are a huge energy draw.

The bank focuses on the customer experience in retail branch design, which, the design team discovered, may inadvertently lead to additional energy use. For example, instead of using a central printer station for multiple tellers, each teller in a typical branch will be provided with a printer at the teller station to speed up the process of printing statements for customers. This approach leads to duplicate printers operating, using electricity, and generating heat. "So, we worked with the design team on solutions— shared printers, encouraging paperless statements and so on— to maintain the customer experience and reduce energy use," offers Faubert.

The bank is also taking this opportunity to use the building design as a way of enhancing the customer experience. "The experience that the bank wanted to bring to its customers was really more of a cozier home-like feel," says Ranadive.

As a result, Intégral is doing a very different lighting design for a bank branch. "Most bank branches are lit like a good corporate office with lots of very even light," explains Ranadive.

"We've really created a branch where you don't have that strict lighting engineering for strict uniformity of light. We've got a lot of table lamps and floor lamps. There's going to be shadows playing off each other. It is going to be really more like your home than the corporate feel."

"It's a little different than anything I've done in the past as an engineer," comments Ranadive, who Faubert calls the unsung hero in the office, an electrical engineer surrounded mostly by mechanical engineers.

The lighting scheme turns out to provide a bonus; it actually helps in reducing the energy use tremendously because they are now putting the light only where it's required. "We're not broadcasting across the whole floor space. It will only be bright where you need it to be bright," says Ranadive. This design gives the customers and staff a lot more control as well. They can turn the lamp on or off in areas where they need more or less light depending on tasks.

"IT MAY NOT BE A VERY SEXY OR ICONIC PROJECT, BUT IN TERMS OF TRUE REPLICABILITY AND ACCELERATION, THIS MODEST 6,000-SQUARE-FOOT, NET ZERO PROTOTYPE IS GOING TO TRAVERSE CANADA IN A WAY THAT HAS WIDE-REACHING EFFECTS ON ENERGY SAVINGS AND CARBON EMISSIONS REDUCTIONS."

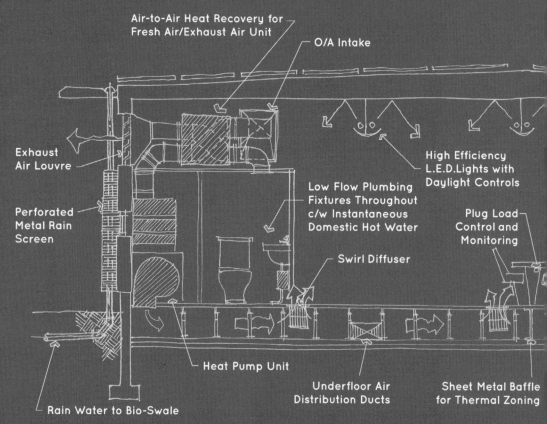

High Performance Roof
Wall and Glazing

Air-to-Air Heat Recovery for
Fresh Air/Exhaust Air Unit

O/A Intake

Exhaust
Air Louvre

High Efficiency
L.E.D.Lights with
Daylight Controls

Low Flow Plumbing
Fixtures Throughout
c/w Instantaneous
Domestic Hot Water

Plug Load
Control and
Monitoring

Perforated
Metal Rain
Screen

Swirl Diffuser

Heat Pump Unit

Rain Water to Bio-Swale

Underfloor Air
Distribution Ducts

Sheet Metal Baffle
for Thermal Zoning

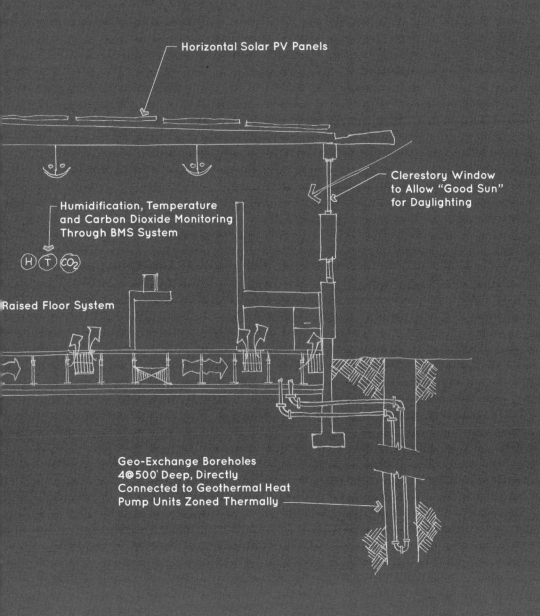

Horizontal Solar PV Panels

Clerestory Window
to Allow "Good Sun"
for Daylighting

Humidification, Temperature
and Carbon Dioxide Monitoring
Through BMS System

(H) (T) (CO₂)

Raised Floor System

Geo-Exchange Boreholes
4@500' Deep, Directly
Connected to Geothermal Heat
Pump Units Zoned Thermally

But it does pose an engineering challenge for Ranadive. "Ten years ago I would come up with a single flat lighting scheme and walk away. It's more interesting, but we are also taking a risk because it's more creative. It's not just numbers anymore; it's really understanding what that light is doing in the space," he comments.

One of the ways the design team figures out the lighting scheme and equipment plug loads is through energy analysis. "It's really important with net zero energy buildings to know how much energy you are going to need not just on a peak but on a yearly use," says Mike Godawa, who is designing the heating and cooling systems for the bank. (The bank will use a geothermal exchange system.)

"We've done a lot of modeling about equipment," he says. Modeling has also been helpful for ensuring they have optimal daylighting and learning when the lights can be off, and then testing the mechanical systems as options. They also tested R-values of the roof and walls to make sure they have the right mix of an energy-efficient envelope with a cost-effective envelope.

"There's that law of diminishing returns where the first inch of insulation does the most...and eventually it gets less and less," Godawa explains. "When you are trying to do a high-performance envelope you want to find that sweet spot where you know how much glass you can use and how much money you can put into the envelope, so we test different glazing systems, mechanical systems, daylighting, overhangs...we tested ventilated façades."

"We really tested the ventilated façades hard to see if it was giving us any value and it really wasn't contributing a lot in this case, so that got value engineered out," Godawa explains.

Another unique mechanism in the bank building is that the delivery system is an Integrated Project Delivery method (IPD). An IPD is a form of contract that differs from the more traditional delivery methods such as lump-sum-tender or design-build or design-assist. IPD is a contractual agreement between the owner, the builder and the designer. With most contracts, there are multiple contracts for different parties. Typically, the owner engages a contractor to build a building.

Separately, the owner engages the design team to design the building. IDP engages the three parties and contractually makes them responsible via some incentives to design the best possible solution. (Google has followed Europe and Canada's lead and has this kind of contract in place for its Living Campus.)

Canada also has public-private partnerships (PPP) primarily for healthcare and education facilities. "This started in Canada because we have a publicly funded healthcare system and the government did not have the money to build brand new facilities," explains Faubert. With these kinds of contracts, the building owner or developer could borrow the money for the buildings and lease it over time, but with some very stringent performance standards on finances, operations, maintenance and energy costs. "Because the contracts are for 25-30 years, they know what the life cycle is on every single piece of equipment and when it's going to be changed," says Faubert. The contract can also incentivize more innovative systems because they don't just focus on life cycle but also on total life cycle costs.

"So, when you look at the five objectives for the bank project, we are all responsible, although not solely in control of any one, for it being net zero, LEED Platinum, etcetera. Because there is a contractual responsibility for us all to work on this together, it ups the ante and is a game changer for the industry."

The net zero bank branch prototype is a challenging little project but an ambitious one. Godawa has seven binders on the bank and he's been on the project for a little over a year. "It's a lot of work," he says.

"I call it the incubator," Faubert says. "We hit on every hurdle, every challenge, every solution. And it's neat, and it's a lot of fun."

The Cost Barrier

An Intégral client at an event at AIA in San Francisco said recently that he hired Intégral for a project because he watched Intégral Founder and CEO Kevin Hydes draw a diagram moving money from the mechanical system to the building envelope. The budget and costs stayed the same, but the energy use in the building dropped dramatically. This is exactly what happened with the Empire State Building and is what RMI's Chief Scientist Amory Lovins calls "tunneling through the cost barrier."

"You work with the money you've got and you move it around. There never is any more money," says Hydes.

Citing cost as an argument against energy efficiency or innovative practices in design is often just an excuse to do something the same, comfortable way it has always been done.

"If it's priced high, it often just means the contractor doesn't know how to do it," says Bradshaw. "A lot of our success comes from how we use our experience to keep the innovative feature in the project." Bradshaw cites the StopWaste.org building, and many others, to show how engineers can call on their experience or simply make an extra effort to show a client a new way that may save money and always, always saves more energy.

On the StopWaste.org building, Intégral staff proposed using a Thermafuser instead of the standard VAV box. (Thermafusers provide optimized temperature settings in different zones of the building, supplying more individualized comfort and greater efficiency than standard Variable Air Volume (VAV) air diffusers which supply constant air flow.)

The contractor, accustomed to installing VAV boxes, greatly over estimated the cost of the Thermafuser and tried to convince the owner to do the less expensive VAV box. The owner had the design team cost out each possibility precisely and it

COST TRANSFER

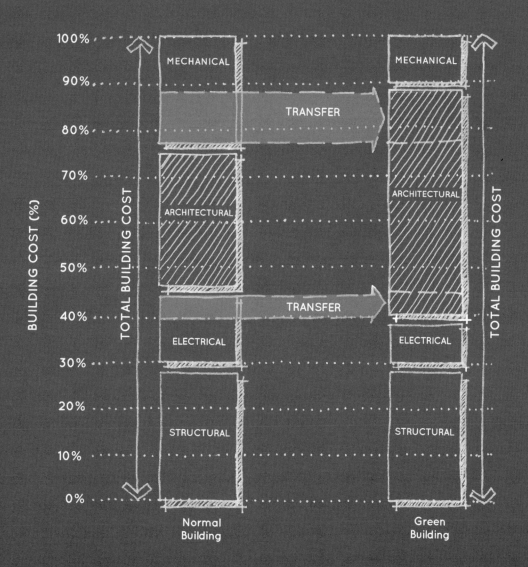

BUILDING COST (%)

100%
90%
80%
70%
60%
50%
40%
30%
20%
10%
0%

TOTAL BUILDING COST

MECHANICAL

TRANSFER

ARCHITECTURAL

TRANSFER

ELECTRICAL

STRUCTURAL

Normal
Building

MECHANICAL

ARCHITECTURAL

ELECTRICAL

STRUCTURAL

Green
Building

TOTAL BUILDING COST

> **"ASKING MORE QUESTIONS, CALLING ON EXPERIENCE OR FINDING SOMEONE WHO HAS EXPERIENCE, AND DIGGING INTO PRECISE COSTS CAN OFTEN MAKE A GOOD CASE FOR THE AFFORDABILITY OF A GREEN FEATURE OR SYSTEM."**

turned out, the Thermafuser came in at slightly less than the VAV box. "The Thermafuser was also much more energy efficient, so it was a win-win," says Bradshaw.

Similarly, Intégral recently worked to install chilled beams in a lab in the Cal Poly Science building. "The contractor came back and said it would take forty hours of labor to install the chilled beams," says Bradshaw. "And so we went and found a contractor who had actually done it, and he said it would take eight hours. We got the contractor to come and explain this to his competitor on the job."

Installing chilled beams in the lab turned out to be slightly less expensive than the proposed alternative as well. That's not always the case. "Sometimes our system is a bit more expensive, but drastically more energy efficient, so they get their money back in three to five years," says Bradshaw. In all cases, Intégral engineers have found, for acceleration to happen, it's better not to accept any initial argument that the greener feature is going to cost more, as that is either a smokescreen and/or an opportunity to educate. Asking more questions, calling on experience or finding someone who has experience, and digging into precise costs can often make a good case for the affordability of a green feature or system.

Acceleration in Silicon Valley

"In terms of accelerating the implementation of sustainability...we've done the first chilled beam, the first radiant system some time ago," says Soladay. "Now it's not the 20-40,000-square-foot test bed, and it's the million square-foot campus in India, in a warm climate, which become examples for areas like Silicon Valley that are conservative in their business approaches, where they don't want to spend a lot of money; they use existing buildings and they work really fast."

"In Silicon Valley the tendency for the last several decades can be described as function follows form," says John Andary, who is working with several developers on new buildings and existing building retrofits in Silicon Valley.

Making a change in a place that is now exploding with development has far-reaching implications for energy and water savings and emission reductions. Yet a building's performance may still be the last thing on the minds of developers in this sector. "The developer mentality in Silicon Valley is not about the building; it's about business: building, selling, leasing space. It's difficult to get a developer to understand this occupancy rate/happy tenant idea. They are about aesthetics," says Andary. Developers in this area want buildings to look a certain way (with lots of glass), and performance is secondary. The trend leaves little room for buildings with any other definition of beauty or character, but Andary doesn't try to change tastes, just energy use.

Andary has made it his mission to give developers the "look" they demand while pushing high performance, even achieving net zero energy performance, in Silicon Valley. Because the developer can make more more money by charging higher rents for these buildings, these higher performing buildings have a good chance to take off and replicate.

Andary is currently working with the developer of the Indio building in Sunnyvale, CA—a core and shell office that went into construction in the summer of 2013—to create a business model for retrofitting inefficient buildings and bringing them to net zero energy. "The developer is very forward thinking and passionate about sustainability. He came to us hoping to develop a business case for creating a

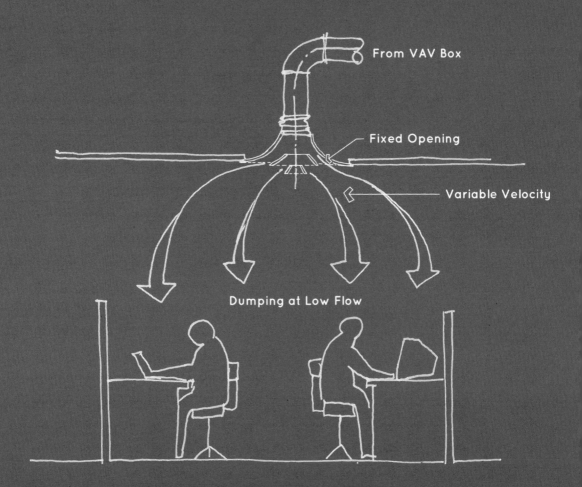

From VAV Box

Fixed Opening

Variable Velocity

Dumping at Low Flow

VAV BOX OPTION

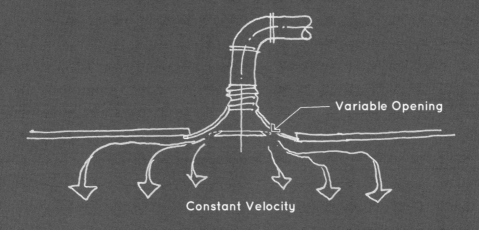

Variable Opening

Constant Velocity

THERMA-FUSER OPTION

net zero energy spec office building out of an existing 30,000-square-foot, 1970s, uninsulated, square building. The developer now has a savvy business case for retrofitting these really, really bad buildings into net zero energy buildings that would take them from Class C- to Class B+, in real estate terms," says Andary. The developer also factored in the savings on energy, smaller sized HVAC equipment, and reduced maintenance due to lower running hours for lights and HVAC equipment to set a budget.

To make it affordable for the Indio building to reach net zero, Andary combined thermal mass and natural ventilation for cooling with a simple Air Conditioning (AC) unit. The walls were uninsulated concrete and Andary convinced the project team to insulate on the outside of the building while exposing the concrete on the inside for greater thermal mass. The thermal mass stores the coolness and releases it during the warmer day. At night, automated windows and skylights open and close on an energy management system to cool the building with outside air.

A simple, cost effective, packaged rooftop HVAC unit brings fresh air in and tempers it, but the building only uses the mechanical system when needed, only about 15 percent of the occupied hours of the year. "Silicon Valley is the perfect climate for zero energy, naturally cool every day of the year," Andary says.

"That's how we met the target of the business case. Normally there would be five times as much air conditioning, so it would be five times as expensive, with additional maintenance costs as well," explains Andary.

The structure of the lease allows the landlord to benefit from net zero energy. The tenant pays a set amount for the lease that includes a set electricity and water cost, not based on usage. So the developer gets to say: "I'm charging them B+ rent but I'm not paying any electricity costs."

"The user experience did drive what we did," says Andary. [See Chapter Two: Perform to read about the User Experience in green design.] Instead of the original dark, dingy building, natural light fills the space. The building is 100 percent daylit, without bringing too much heat in.

"We refined our skylight design into a fourth generation design by incorporating a very low cost, prismatic acrylic diffusing lens to soften and spread the direct beam sunlight being harvested by the skylights," says Kaneda. "We are using glass on just 2.5 percent of the roof area to get daylight into the building, yet we expect the building to use just one-tenth of the lighting energy of an office standard building."

When electric lights go on in the evening or on cloudy days they will be high efficiency LEDs and if any daylight is available the lights will efficiently dim to augment the daylight with electric light.

Occupants can open and close windows and skylights for comfort. Ceiling fans provide occupants another level of comfort control before they turn on the air conditioning. Desk fans and plug strips with occupancy sensors are issued as part of the lease. Each tenant has an energy target in the lease. If they can't manage to it, they pay extra. If they beat it, they get money back. In true Silicon Valley high-tech style, the design team is also creating an app for the building so people can track their energy use.

The most significant thing about the project is not so much that it transformed a really bad building to a net zero building and changed a dark dingy building to a pleasant, naturally lit building, but it's the fact that the developer and design team recently got a grant from the state of California to do the exact same thing to the building next door. "This tiny project means so much," says Andary. "The key to accelerating net zero in Silicon Valley is coming up with a business model that makes it affordable." Acceleration happens when replication takes care of itself.

"High-tech startups could get excited about this. Any developer could buy into this concept. This business model is not about getting a payback over time. It's about getting higher rent and making money immediately," says Andary. "That's why it is a great model to transition this sector." This model is powerful because it flips the old story that green buildings take upfront sacrifice and patience to be worth it (a scarcity model), and now, through applying experience and innovation, it is immediately providing significant value as well as long-term value (an abundance model).

A number of Silicon Valley high-tech companies are now doing their first from the ground up buildings. As Andary began to work with developers of these buildings, he said to himself: "I am going to crack the code on big glass buildings with no operable windows and do it cost effectively."

On the Clyde Avenue building, a developer office building in Mountainview, CA, Andary and the design team showed they could use off-the-shelf technology, be clever with it, and achieve energy efficiency at no extra cost. The main reason they succeeded: For the first time it is affordable to install very high-performance glass at an affordable price. (The trend toward lots of glass is not going away anytime soon, Andary notes.) And for the first time in history, it is cheaper to add PV to the building than to add more HVAC.

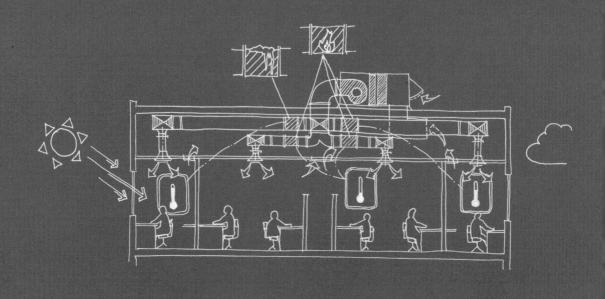

THERMODYNAMIC ZONES

The city of Mountainview wanted to incentivize developers to build to a higher level of performance. The city had previously mandated LEED Gold. Now they offered an incentive for going higher, giving a higher floor area ratio to anyone who reaches Platinum. (Just what developers want.)

The Clyde Avenue building already had a building design drawn when the incentive appeared. The developer asked Intégral to help meet the LEED Platinum goal, but with the existing design. According to Andary the building had a challenging lay out for high performance, with deep floor plates, poor orientation for passive design, and lots of glass. "It's hard to get performance out of the glass," he says.

Aside from the constraints of the design, the developer did not want to spend a lot of extra money to hit Platinum. And, for the sake of attracting future tenants, the developer did not want the building to have an unusual character. "We needed to take simple off-the-shelf HVAC systems and be clever about how we used them to hit a target of 48 percent energy cost savings to get maximum LEED points," Andary explains.

The team started with the envelope, taking off the decorative architectural features and making them functional for shading, all at a negligible cost. For the building's HVAC, the design team used the same off-the-shelf packaged rooftop unit the developer had in the original drawing and budget, but in a more creative way to save energy.

To maximize the energy savings and comfort from the HVAC, Andary employed something he calls thermodynamic zoning. Once the envelope of the building was enhanced to lower energy use, the HVAC cooling loads became significantly smaller. At this point it became cost effective to use five HVAC units instead of two, which is the traditional Silicon Valley VAV design approach. The five thermodynamic zones represent the four external solar orientations (north, east, south and west) plus the interior. Because the need for cooling is relatively consistent in each thermodynamic zone, it is possible to use outside air for much more of the year. In the Silicon Valley climate, that represents a 59 percent HVAC energy savings.

127

The HVAC got them to 30 percent savings with no extra costs. They still had 18 percent savings to go to reach their goal. According to Andary, normally to get the extra savings they would have to change the glass, change the building, or do something more radical with the HVAC that would be more expensive. Using this approach, it would have cost an additional $10 million to get the additional savings they needed.

But they installed PV on two parking decks instead, which made it affordable to get the extra savings. "Lo and behold, because of radical reductions in costs, installing PV was cheaper than changing the architecture or the HVAC," says Andary.

"This is what I would call a tipping point," he says. "This is the first time that has ever happened on any project I've worked on. This is a game changer. PV has always been more expensive. It has always been cheaper to do a better HVAC or change the architecture." Adding PV got them to 48 percent energy savings and LEED Platinum. "PV was absolutely the most cost-effective way to meet the goal," Andary says.

In addition, the standard HVAC is easy to maintain. The PV panels are also easy to maintain. Essentially, maintenance on the building is cost free.

"We're getting 48 percent energy savings at slightly less cost than building to the standard ASHRAE compliant code," says Andary. The lesson: You can take standard equipment and use it in a creative way plus benefit from the tipping point of lower costs of PV and high-performance glass.

So, this story is about a design team being innovative and it is about performance, but it's really about making high performance affordable and accelerating low energy design, especially since the systems are all off the shelf. The Clyde Avenue developer anticipates that his project will be the first developer-led, large-scale office project in Silicon Valley to reach LEED Platinum certification, leading the way for others to do the same.

"To make these high performance buildings for the dollars they [developers] expect is something we have been working toward for a long period of time. Making it affordable and cost effective is part of a sustainable project," notes Andary.

Value vs. Cost

A number of cost studies in the last ten years have attempted to determine the exact premium of building green. Lisa Fay Matthiessen has conducted some of the most well-known of those studies.

While heading up international consultant Davis Langdon's sustainability group, Matthiessen and Peter Morris co-authored *"Understanding the Cost of Green."* Intended initially as an internal study comparing the costs of green vs. non-green buildings, they presented the report publicly at the AIA National Convention in 2004, and it quickly gained attention across the industry. "Rather than looking at the additive costs for green—if I add green elements to my building, how much more money do I need?— the study looks at overall construction costs, measured in terms of dollars per square foot," explains Matthiessen. The study compares green and non-green projects to see whether there is a statistically significant cost difference between the two. This approach changed the conversation about sustainability costs, and allowed the industry to understand that sustainability is typically not a primary cost factor on most projects, and that most projects manage to achieve sustainability within budget parameters. While those in the forefront of the industry had known this for a while, the *"Understanding the Cost of Green"* report allowed the rank and file to overcome their suspicions and fears about cost.

They followed up the original report with an update in 2007 and Morris and Matthiessen are currently working on the third installment of the Cost of Green series, teaming with BNIM Architects and other leading design firms. "This 2013 report is well underway, and the authors have data on more than 200 'Next-Generation Green' projects—projects that are targeting the very highest sustainability goals: Living Building, Net-Zero, and LEED Platinum," says Matthiessen. "Initial statistical analysis shows that LEED Silver and even Gold have become competitive in terms of cost, while costs for the Next-Generation projects are all over the map; some cost more than typical buildings, and some do not."

Once complete, the Cost of Green 2013 report will delve into construction costs in detail, looking at correlations between costs for separate building systems and components and how those relate to level of green. And the report will look at building performance over time, as related to cost, using both statistical analysis and case studies.

How we measure costs is quite complicated. There can be first costs, life-cycle costs, triple bottom line costs, and somehow figuring the cost of well-being. Despite the nebulous nature of cost determination, Matthiessen says she can draw a few conclusions from her extensive work evaluating costs of green design. Namely, due to what she calls the "product development cycle," we can say costs of green are definitely coming down.

There are reasons— beyond more off the shelf, affordable technologies— for the lower costs on the higher performance buildings. Matthiessen explains, "If you are doing a net zero building and generating your own energy, you end up working hard to reduce the costs of your mechanical systems so you can pay for the added costs of PV. There's this sort of paradox that if you are only setting out to reduce your energy use by 20 percent you might not actually be as thorough and diligent as you would be if you were going for net zero. Those projects that have a higher goal are probably doing a better job of cost control."

Intégral and the green design world can point to many buildings where they managed to push the building to the highest performing standards, including net zero, on a standard budget.

"Where there's a will, there's a way," Rumsey likes to say. The Missouri Department of Natural Resources (MODNR) was one of the earliest ones Intégral staff worked on that proved this case, and many have followed.

Completed in 2008, the first state office building in the United States to be awarded a LEED Platinum rating by the USGBC, MODNR was one of the first to show it is possible to do a Platinum building on a standard budget. (Both McLennan and Rumsey worked on the building.)

Now LEED Platinum is common enough and affordable enough that there is a push to make Platinum a part of the building code in many places, like Santa Monica for example. Around 2006, many municipalities had already begun requiring new buildings to be LEED Silver. Many of them hit Gold in the following years and now the push is on for Platinum. These certifications play a significant role in the

"PEOPLE THINK THAT THE CEILING HAS BEEN SET [AT LEED PLATINUM] AND IT'S AN ARTIFICIAL CEILING. PEOPLE WILL ONLY JUMP AS HIGH AS THE CEILING. SO WE'VE LIFTED THE ROOF OFF THE CEILING. AND NOW WE HAVE PROJECTS ALL OVER THE WORLD THAT ARE GOING MUCH FURTHER THAN ANYONE THOUGHT WAS POSSIBLE JUST A COUPLE OF YEARS AGO. AND THAT CHANGES EVERYTHING. IT MAKES LEED MORE ACHIEVABLE THAN PEOPLE EVER THOUGHT."

acceleration of green buildings, and our ability to achieve them keeps rising up. Many in deep green design who spend their time on net zero and Living Buildings think of Platinum as the least of what we can do now. And we need to do so much more.

McLennan makes it his life's purpose to remind us of the reality of how far we need to go. His reality checks are only tempered by his dauntless belief that we are completely capable of getting there.

"People think that the ceiling has been set [at LEED Platinum] and it's an artificial ceiling," McLennan explains. "People will only jump as high as the ceiling. So we've lifted the roof off the ceiling. And now we have projects all over the world that are going much further than anyone thought was possible just a couple of years ago. And that changes everything. It makes LEED more achievable than people ever thought."

Standards and Acceleration

McLennan created the Living Building Challenge (LBC), a certification program that covers development at all scales, in 2005 and launched it with the Cascadia Green Building Council in 2006. The Challenge is now administered by the International Living Future Institute, of which McLennan is also the CEO.

The Living Building Challenge covers seven performance areas: Site, Water, Energy, Health, Materials, Equity and Beauty and "defines the most advanced measure of sustainability in the built environment possible today," according to the Challenge's own stipulations.

One of the key mechanisms that separates LBC from other standards is measurement. There is a huge variation in terms of performance in LEED-certified buildings. Some of them are energy hogs and some of them are very efficient. Some of them are wasteful with water and some of them are not. And that's a problem, according to McLennan. Buildings need to have at least a year's worth of data to be certified as a Living Building.

McLennan sees transparency as a positive trend in building standards. The Living Building Challenge has promoted transparency, both of materials and performance, through monitoring and through labeling. ILFI's Declare label is an ingredients label for building products and its new JUST label measures social equity. In October 2013, Intégral Group was the first firm to be awarded a JUST label. While Living Building Challenge has brought transparency to more buildings, the Challenge itself is often criticized for not being affordable or reachable by most building owners. McLennan argues that the Living Building Challenge highlights systemic things that need to change, including changing the economic framework for how we value building. "It's a lot cheaper when you externalize costs on to society. LBC is accounting for its own externalities and addressing them, and that requires an investment up front," he says. "In many ways we are simply further along the innovation curve with Living Buildings. People gave the same argument with LEED until recently and each year Living Buildings become more affordable."

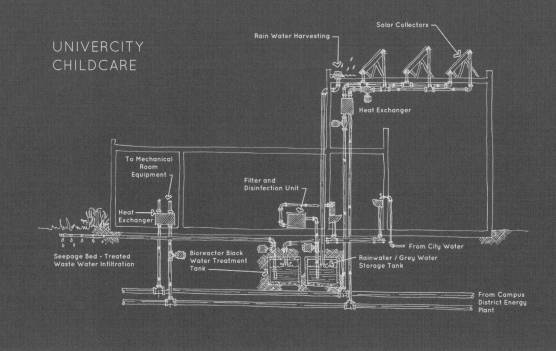

Solar Collectors

Rain Water Harvesting

Heat Exchanger

To Mechanical
Room
Equipment

Filter and
Disinfection Unit

Heat
Exchanger

Seepage Bed - Treated
Waste Water Infiltration

Bioreactor Black
Water Treatment
Tank

From City Water

Rainwater / Grey Water
Storage Tank

From Campus
District Energy
Plant

A Living Building on a Budget

Intégral Group has worked on several Living Buildings and, in fact, has done one, the UniverCity ChildCare building at Simon Fraser University (SFU) in Burnaby, British Columbia, that came in on a standard fixed budget.

Meeting the technical requirements of LBC—to generate all energy on-site and export any excess and to capture all the building's water and treat all wastewater on-site—on a standard budget, makes this building a realistic and replicable model and defies this commonly repeated idea that a Living Building is always an out of reach and widely inaccessible project.

"It is so simple, so natural, so elegant," says the building's project manager, Jean-Sebastien Tessier, of the 5,690 square-foot facility, the daytime home of about fifty children, three-to five years old. "It is a very passively designed building and the only special features that we added to meet the LBC were the solar array and the (black) water treatment system," says Tessier. The rest was simply good design and construction practices.

133

The school follows the Reggio Emilia approach to education, which focuses on exploration and discovery with a special emphasis on the physical environment, meaning the building and the landscape and surrounding community.

What's better than playing in a trench of water when you are a Reggio Emilia kid? Rainwater captured from the roof of your daycare and flowing down a channel around the playground. "It rains frequently in Vancouver," says Tessier, "so the children can build dams and play in the water and learn about water." They have no idea that they are in a Living Building at their age, but that doesn't mean it won't change them to be there, to play in captured rainwater and climb on a hill beside a solar collector array. But their parents and teachers and local community members do know and it's influencing a whole sea change around it.

UniverCity Childcare

Going outside is a big part of the learning experience at SFU and it also became part of the systems, says Tessier. (The area occupied by the landscape is more than 70 percent of the total site, which shows the importance of the relationship to the outdoors.) The design team determined the number of air changes in certain rooms based on the frequency of children exiting the room to play outside. The community room, for example, needs no mechanical ventilation since children open windows and doors often. "The building is a living organism with living occupants," Tessier explains.

Other ways children influenced the design: trickle vents and passive ventilation limit drafts and noise in the nap room and other quieter areas. The radiant system is warm, comfortable and quiet. Windows are low to the floor so kids get the views and the breeze on their level. (Lesson learned: Kids will try to climb on, and possibly break, ventilation grilles if you put them low to the floor where they can most benefit from the air.)

The building was the first in the vicinity to link into a district heat system being planned at the time the team designed the childcare center. In the summer, the facility's solar thermal system produces much more hot water than it needs. "We decided we would have a greater impact by sharing the energy and by taking the hot water from the solar panels and sending it into the system for other buildings around us," Tessier explains. Now all the buildings in the UniverCity vicinity must connect to the district system.

"It's a fairly simple system. We use the district energy system as a source of energy with a radiant heating system and the ventilation is displacement with heat recovery. Building orientation and space planning was at the heart of the energy discussions. Careful space planning allowed very little ductwork, thus fewer materials," says Tessier.

The facility is built from local resources and free of toxic materials that damage developing bodies and brains and the majority of construction waste was diverted from local landfills.

"It is very replicable and cost wasn't a factor," says Tessier. The project was completed for about $3.2 million, which is approximately 15 percent less than the average cost of building a traditional childcare facility, and will have lower operating costs than conventional childcare centers. There were no serious budget constraints placed on it to make it an "affordable" Living Building. It happened naturally, because the best building was a passive building. The best building was simple and elegant.

The childcare centre is one of the first projects Intégral is measuring as part of its Performance Engineering tracking tool. (LBC also requires basic monitoring of performance for one year.) "We are finding that the building has great performance," says Tessier.

A blackwater treatment facility and on-site infiltration of stormwater are also components of the strategy to meet the Living Building Challenge net zero water Imperative.

The rainwater and blackwater systems are similar to another Living Building in Vancouver, the VanDusen Botanical Garden Visitor Center. In fact, many of the systems in VanDusen are similar: radiant heating, natural ventilation via operable windows, a heat recovery unit. By contrast, however, this 20,000-square-foot Living Building came in at $21.9 million. (Most of the cost is from unique architectural features and not the mechanical or energy systems, however.)

Like the childcare centre, all water is retained on-site and treated on-site through buried percolation by a prefab bacteria unit. A green roof feeds a rainwater catchment system below grade. A highly visible PV array serves the commercial kitchen and solar collectors on an adjacent existing building heat water. Excess heat is dumped into the ground for recharging the geo-exchange field that feeds the ground source heat pumps.

The architect, Perkins+Will, chose to build with local resources, including lots of wood. The building's organic shape and texture blends into surrounding trees. Every piece of wood in the roof is a different size and shape and each beam is made uniquely. The curvy prefabricated roof was placed on in one piece, with an oculus as its centerpiece drawing air from outside. Overhangs slope outward to serve as a design feature and optimize daylight and cooling and LED lighting integrates seamlessly into the beautiful yet subtle structure.

An Exemplary Living Building

It is in every way a completely different Living Building than UniverCity Childcare. VanDusen is not meant to be replicable "just like you wouldn't replicate the Sydney Opera House," McLennan explains. It's more of an inspiring ideal. Still, ideals accelerate the transformation of attitudes about what is possible. Inspiring buildings bring more·exposure. VanDusen increased visitors by 30 percent in the first year after the new building opened, according to Goran Ostojic, the engineer of record for the project.

The VanDusen Botanical Garden is in the heart of Vancouver, an almost Olmsted-like retreat from urban life, a center of botany, horticulture and environmental learning. With 55 acres of gardens, 255,000 plants from around the world reside

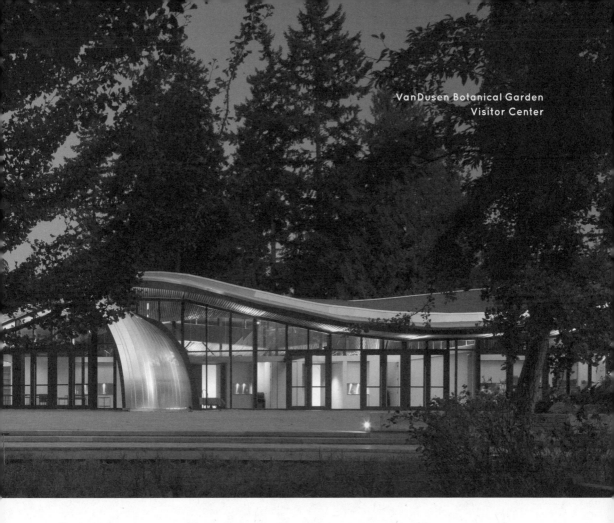

in a pastoral landscape scattered with forests, water and rocks and with distant views of the mountains and Vancouver cityscape.

The VanDusen project started as a small renovation. "The Vancouver Parks Board then decided they wanted to make an example, and then there was the political will to create something big," says Ostojic.

Basically, they said, "Do whatever you can imagine."

"As designers we always imagine. We always dream. There are always quite a few things we want to implement," he muses. The interesting thing for Ostojic was the process. His team came up with a lot of possibilities, including

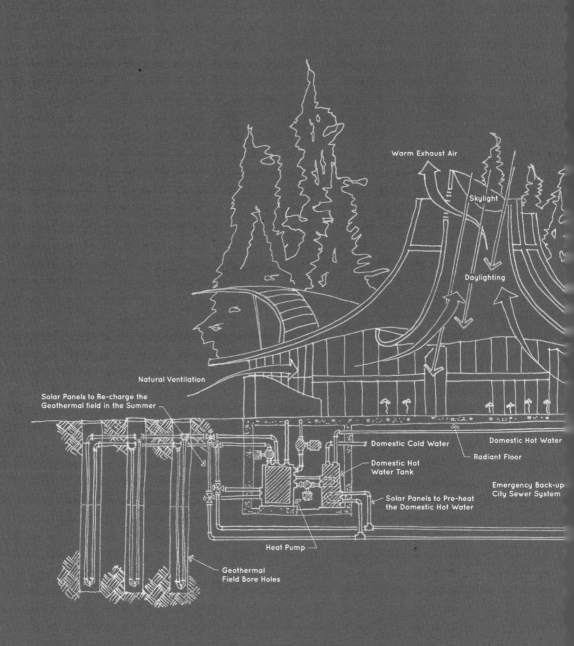

Warm Exhaust Air

Skylight

Daylighting

Natural Ventilation

Solar Panels to Re-charge the
Geothermal field in the Summer

Domestic Cold Water

Domestic Hot Water

Domestic Hot
Water Tank

Radiant Floor

Emergency Back-up
City Sewer System

Solar Panels to Pre-heat
the Domestic Hot Water

Heat Pump

Geothermal
Field Bore Holes

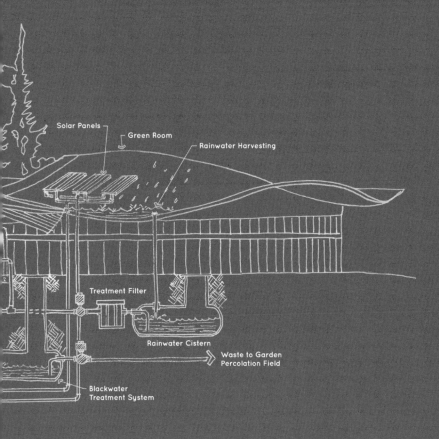

Solar Panels

Green Room

Rainwater Harvesting

Treatment Filter

Rainwater Cistern

Waste to Garden
Percolation Field

Blackwater
Treatment System

anaerobic digesters, and they did extensive life-cycle analysis and modeling to justify different possibilities.

"Then there was a budget problem so the project went on hold. Then, when the project restarted, the Parks Board decided to make it Canada's first Living Building," he recalls. "We were like, what's a Living Building?"

The time constraints and the budget constraints forced integrated design. "When you have all these issues and very little time to solve them, it causes people to integrate. These multiple goals could be reached only if we all worked together."

The power of modeling was important to make the case for various features, he emphasizes. "This was the first time our office did not do LEED energy modeling." Living Building Challenge modeling, for example, requires you to actually find out how many people are going to use the projectors so we know if we can make net zero energy use, he explains. "ASHRAE energy modeling is a hypothetical formula. This is the real world. Usually, as long as we have more capacity than load, the client is happy. Not with this building." (They are now monitoring the performance of the building as part of the requirements for LBC. The data will appear on a screen in the lobby for visitors to see.)

The team also thought of a creative hands-on learning game where children could participate in a biomass heating process, gathering wood from trees that had to be cut on the property. But they could not implement the idea due to the constraints of the Challenge.

"Jason said no combustion," Ostojic laments with a smile.

"Usually rating systems push things forward. In this case, the rating system was an obstacle to doing what was sustainable for the site," Ostojic says.

McLennan defends the Living Building approach: "They have a project that now has no emissions as compared to one that would have emissions. There is no risk of fire, no risk of explosions or accidents, no air quality issues, and no need to constantly truck in biomass that would add more traffic and create more pollution. There is simply no comparison between a solar building with

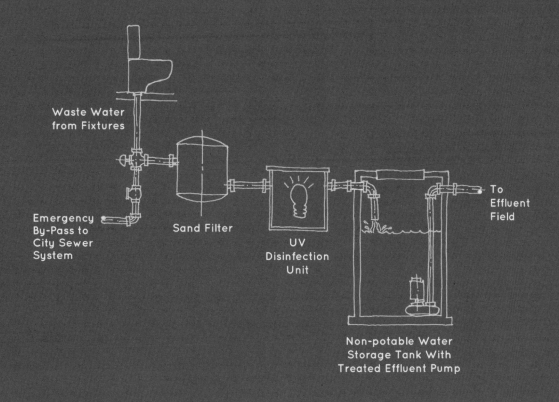

Waste Water
from Fixtures

Emergency
By-Pass to
City Sewer
System

Sand Filter

UV
Disinfection
Unit

To
Effluent
Field

Non-potable Water
Storage Tank With
Treated Effluent Pump

no moving parts getting energy from the sun and even the best biomass system with fuel —even if waste products were brought in."

The registered Living Building required a lot of effort, coordination and some headaches, but it turned out really nicely," says Ostojic.

VanDusen has been hailed by *Fast Company* and others as one of the ten most innovative buildings in the world. "Vancouver is small, but it is an important recognition for us," Ostojic says. "It shows you the power of sustainability."

Innovation to Replication

It's obviously much easier for building owners and design teams to follow the SFU's UniverCity model than the VanDusen model. The VanDusen building and other highly innovative projects, Living Building Challenge or net zero projects, create opportunities to blaze new trails, to innovate. These very special projects often have a very special client or a bigger budget.

"A special project allows you to be the first. It's allowing you to try things that are uncommon, allowing you to make mistakes. Then you learn," says McLennan. **"Once you have that experience, you begin to be able to replicate and you do not need the perfect client, the perfect site, the perfect project."**

While VanDusen is aiming to be a Living Building that allowed unique innovation opportunities and influences a crowd, the UniverCity Childcare Centre's standard budget provides an example of how innovations lead to replication.

"One of the things about Intégral is that these are people who have been doing cutting edge stuff for a long time, so they are able to leap frog over the learning curve," says McLennan. "Experience matters. Experience at the edge matters if you want the edge to become the norm."

McLennan tells a great story about a team in Seattle that created their own edge, innovated, and then went on to replicate. In 2009, a couple of young architects, Stacy Smedley and Chris Hellstern, associates in the Seattle office of KMD Architects, attended the Living Future conference, or 'unconference' as it is known. They were inspired by what they heard there and they really wanted to do a Living Building, but they didn't have any clients who wanted to do one.

The only way they could think of to get a client was to offer to meet the requirements of the Challenge at no extra cost. They found a willing client, Seattle's Bertschi School, a private school about to do an addition. The leadership at KMD allowed them to donate their time and services and they convinced all the project team to donate their time and services. (Intégral did not work on the project.)

THE IDEA

THE PROTOTYPE

REPLICATION

The school's PV system and efficient envelope allow it to come in at net zero. A river of rainwater runs through one room and a living wall also thrives inside the school. The quality of the indoor environment certainly affects learning in a positive way, and the school now teaches the principles of the LBC.

According to KMD's website, "Since the Bertschi School's inception, KMD Architects has been convincing manufacturers to offer or switch to healthier, more environmentally friendly products. Currently, KMD is rewriting specifications to eliminate toxic materials from their projects."

"The Bertschi School allowed these young architects to practice on the edge on a small enough project that it didn't bankrupt any of the consultants who donated time. And suddenly, these really young designers were one of the first designers in the world to have designed and built a Living Building," says McLennan, who supported the team through the process of creating the Living Building. The project recently became the world's fourth fully certified Living Building. KMD changed some of its practices and is also getting more jobs that call on expertise with net zero or regenerative design.

Soon after, one of the architects on the school project started her own business, Sprout! Collective, to reinvent the portable classroom to meet Living Building

Bertschi School

standards. Changes in the practices at the architecture firm, changes in the curriculum of the school and the evolution of a career to reproduce portable classrooms as Living Building classrooms—this is moving from innovation to replication on a number of levels. This is acceleration.

The Living Building Challenge is also learning and changing all the time—a living tool, which is becoming more holistic, says McLennan. When it launched, it was the first standard to incorporate beauty. In the latest version of the Standard, the Challenge added an equity stipulation for social justice. Now they are expanding typologies and certifying things that move, like ships.

"What we are really trying to do right now is demonstrate that this is something that can be achieved by every building type in every climate zone in every country in the world," says McLennan. "There's nothing like seeing an actual project to demystify myths about how much something is going to cost, or what it's going to look like or how it's going to perform. It tends to create its own field of dreams."

"ONE OF THE THINGS ABOUT INTÉGRAL IS THAT THESE ARE PEOPLE WHO HAVE BEEN DOING CUTTING EDGE STUFF FOR A LONG TIME, SO THEY ARE ABLE TO LEAP FROG OVER THE LEARNING CURVE."

SUSTAIN

SFU Living Neighborhood

04

We can build one green building at a
time, or we can design our communities
to be resilient and sustaining by seeing
them as connected to each other,
to neighborhoods, to infrastructure and,
of course, to the environment.

— Kevin Hydes, Founder and CEO Intégral Group

Sustain

"In my lifetime, the population has gone from 2 billion people to more than 7 billion people. We've also gone from 325 parts per million of carbon in standard air to more than 392 parts per million, well above what scientists tell us is the safe upper limit for carbon in our atmosphere," reflects Hydes.

"When we talk about climate change we talk about two things," Hydes explains. "We talk about mitigation, which is using less. On the other side is adaptation, which is what we are going to need to do knowing that we already have climate change happening. "We can't take our foot off the mitigate pedal, but for adaptation we need a new breed of leadership and learning by everyone in the industry. In our firm, it's where we have to put the most effort in next."

"What we are doing as a firm is trying to help get off the bad drug, which is fossil fuel," says Hydes. "So, we pursue and promote lower energy, cleaner energy, zero energy, regenerative buildings, and they just need to become the standard, quickly, quickly. As our understanding of the issues continues to evolve along with our ability to influence larger and different patterns, our organization evolves our services to focus more on Living Buildings, sustainable sites and ecodistricts. This is what we mean when we say sustain."

As Hurricane Sandy bore down on New York and New Jersey in 2012, about to raise awareness around issues of resilience in a very personal way for millions of Americans, Hydes thought back to a less tragic awakening experience of his own a few years earlier.

On Thursday, August 14, 2003, when a massive power outage struck the Northeastern U.S., the Midwest and Ontario, Hydes was visiting Ottawa, where the outage lasted five days. Traffic lights did not work and finding food was a challenge because refrigeration was down. But he managed to stay cooler than many people in Ottawa during those warm summer days without air conditioning. "I went to the old historic hotel with operable windows in downtown Ottawa," he explains. Simply put, passive cooling is more resilient.

"If you live in a really cold climate like the Arctic and lose power, how long does it take for the building to really cool down? If you are in a resilient building, it should take a long, long time," Hydes explains. "It should be like a thermos that protects. And it needs to be designed so that it never cools down so much that pipes break and people freeze. And then if you were in a really hot climate and lost power how long would it take the building to heat up? That might be more like a flower. You'd want the thing to open up and just let its heat out and then stay cool enough to protect people from heat stroke."

This concept of a building or community that can still operate when its power, heating, and water systems fail is also often called passive survivability, a term coined by journalist and green design expert Alex Wilson that planners and designers are using more and more in the face of events like Hurricane Sandy.

Olympic Village

Resilience Pushes Sustainability

We may not be prepared for climate change, but resilience has been part of architecture and infrastructure in areas vulnerable to earthquakes for some time. A major fault line runs all the way up the western coast of the United States and Canada. In California, people are biding their time until the big one hits. Hotels, public buildings and transit stations all post visible signage providing guidance for coping with earthquakes. Vancouver also expects and waits for the big one. Law requires resilience to be literally built into new buildings in Vancouver for the safety and protection of its people, but old buildings are not all up to speed.

Stuart Hood is currently working on two buildings in Vancouver—an airport emergency services building and the new headquarters for the Royal Canadian Mounted Police (RCMP)— that are driven largely by the issue of resilience, both high on the passive survivability index.

The airport building needs to be resilient because it will be the headquarters for any operations that need to occur during an emergency such as an earthquake. It's an efficient building that incorporates geothermal exchange and rainwater harvesting. In this case, the resilience factor is what pushed sustainability. "If their utility plant goes down when an earthquake happens and you are required to operate this thing disconnected from the grid, you have to think very differently about the systems you put in it. Typically, it ends up being what we would have previously called a 'sustainable' solution," explains Hood.

Hood's other large resiliency project at the moment, home and headquarters to Canada's famous Royal Canadian Mounted Police, is a 24-7, high-security operation, which would also be the operational hub for a local disaster. All the utilities have to keep running all the time. "It has to be resilient and redundant. You can't rely on natural gas because an earthquake may sever the natural gas main. Instead, you need an all-electric (heat pump) solution that can be backed up by on-site generators," explains Hood.

"THIS RESILIENT AND REDUNDANT APPROACH IS THE EXCEPTION RATHER THAN THE NORM, BUT AS WE GRAPPLE WITH THE EFFECTS OF CLIMATE CHANGE AND INCREASED PRESSURE ON OUR RESOURCES, WE MAY LOOK TO CITIES ON FAULT LINES AND TRADITIONALLY IN THE PATH OF HURRICANES THAT HAVE MORE EXPERIENCE PLANNING FOR DISASTER."

This resilient and redundant approach is the exception rather than the norm, but as we grapple with the effects of climate change and increased pressure on our resources, we may look to cities on fault lines and traditionally in the path of hurricanes that have more experience planning for disaster.

"Building today in most of our major cities, there's flooding, water issues, and increased forest fire issues. There are also the demands population increases will put on energy, water and food throughout the world. What we'll be doing as a profession is a lot more risk assessment and risk management," predicts Hydes.

Reliable and Efficient:
District Systems

"How are we going to cope with climate change?" asks Trevor Butler. "Are we going to go for smaller scale electricity generation systems and putting PV on rooftops? I think we are going to see a lot more decentralized plants because of the drive toward a low carbon economy and climate change."

These systems will help us weather the storms and help us prevent them because they are low carbon and emit fewer greenhouse gas emissions, the beginning of the vicious cycle of climate change. "It might be a natural disaster or some kind of impact from climate change, but the grid is not reliable. Current modern infrastructure is not resilient," says Hydes. "This is where green communities and self-sustaining networks really come up."

"By making your own electricity on-site it is possible to save between 30-100 percent of carbon emissions compared to grid-derived power," says Butler, who got his start working with district systems in his native England, where district and microdistrict systems are much more common. "The primary energy source for electrical generation is most commonly fossil fuels combusted to drive turbines, with the residual lower grade heat thrown away in cooling towers. With combined heat and power you generate electricity on a smaller scale and the heat is collected and then piped around the development, therefore getting a net efficiency of 80 percent out of the primary energy fuels."

A typical coal-fired power station operates at 35 percent efficiency. Plus, all the distribution transformers reduce efficiency even further with the end result being that electricity used in our buildings is only 28 percent efficient by the time it is used. Using his current home of Canada as an example, Butler explains the desirability of CHP systems depends on where you are. "In a high carbon content electric grid like Alberta, Saskatchewan or Nova Scotia, they burn coal and throw heat away. When you go to British Columbia, Manitoba or Quebec the grid is pretty much all hydro electric. CHP doesn't make as much sense there because the grid is so clean."

The reasons for district systems, according to Butler, include net fossil fuel and carbon efficiency and shared resources. In downtown Vancouver, for example, there is one central steam plant that is operating at full efficiency all the time, instead of 100 buildings with 100 small-scale boilers that kick in and out. This approach optimizes efficiency.

You can share energy between buildings with a central thermal plant. Some buildings require heating all year (hotels, hospitals, residences) and some, like offices, have high cooling needs. In a district system, you can take the heat from the ones with too much heat and give it to the ones who need it.

Some small-scale or "microdistrict" examples of the systems Butler is talking about include Telus Towers and SoLo district, both in British Columbia. Some larger developments include the Olympic Village in Vancouver and the redevelopment of the Walter Reed army base in Washington, D.C. Even more ambitious examples of district projects, such as the Summit Bechtel Reserve in Glen Jean, West Virginia and the Simon Fraser University campus in British Columbia, will operate at net zero carbon and energy. Not only does thinking on a district scale address issues of resilience, it makes sense when it comes to costs as well as energy savings.

"Maybe alongside the push for net zero buildings, we should think about a district energy plan that is net zero," comments Kaneda, referring to the California Energy Code that requires all new commercial buildings in the state to be net zero by 2030. An executive order requires the same thing of all federal buildings by 2030. This policy promotes scaling up, but is still designed around the one building at a time idea.

Kaneda admits he spends a lot of time thinking about the California Energy Code requirements and how to innovate beyond them, since many of his net zero practices are now becoming standard. "The total cost for California would be less to put in a district system than all net zero buildings," he says. And when it comes to high-rise buildings, California will likely have to offset energy use because net zero in a high rise is too expensive or might not be possible.

This concept is what McLennan refers to as "scale jumping." In a properly sized district system, the cost of infrastructure gets spread out so there is not a burden on any one project and it's not so huge that the system itself is cumbersome, bulky and expensive. "We envision communities that have these decentralized networks of district-scale infrastructure punctuated by building-scale infrastructure," says McLennan.

"You then end up with an incredible diversity and you end up with a city where you would never lose all your power. You would never have a city that would have the problems of failure of water systems, sewage and so on, because there's more diversity and resilience built into the system," he explains.

Symbiosis: Telus Towers and SoLo District

Telus Towers in downtown Vancouver shows how we can begin to connect infrastructure on a small scale. The two towers, one previously existing and one new, will reside in symbiotic relation to each other. An existing data center that serves all of British Columbia gives off waste heat that is pumped through a geothermal exchange system to heat the adjacent half-million-square-foot new office building. We don't necessarily need new construction to accomplish this feat. The data center is quite old, says Conrad Schartau. In fact, the design team even found old wires from the 1920s in the building.

While Telus Towers is two buildings, SoLo District in Burnaby, B.C., is a mini neighborhood energy scheme with offices, residential and retail spaces that applies some of the same concepts and systems. Four high-rise towers will house 1800 residential units in the SoLo District.

"Essentially we've got a district energy system with a geothermal field," says Schartau. The residential space is all air-conditioned using the waste heat from the retail and the office spaces and it's a completely shared energy system, using variable refrigerant flow connected to a hydronic ambient loop and geothermal exchange.

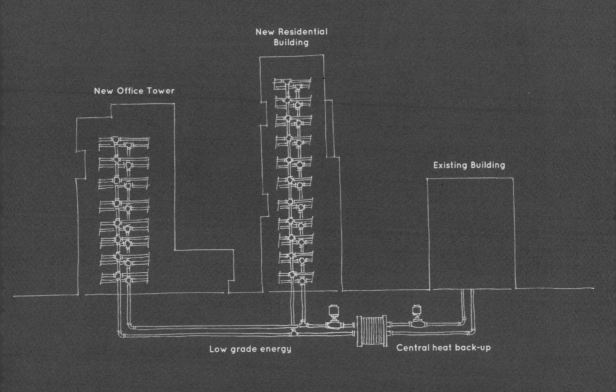

New Residential Building

New Office Tower

Existing Building

Low grade energy

Central heat back-up

TELUS WASTE-HEAT LOOP

"There are not many of those systems on the planet. What most people do is when one unit is heating they send the cooling to atmosphere and vice versa. The geothermal loop captures the heat in the water. And this was done for the same price as a regular AC system. This is like buying a Ferrari for the price of a BMW," says Schartau.

The SoLo District will undergo monitoring, measurement and verification through Intégral's Performance Engineering program. Information Intégral gathers from the performance engineering process may be fed back in to improve SoLo District performance and it may affect the way Intégral and other firms approach similar systems on other projects to reach for even greater performance. (See the Perform chapter for more information on Performance Engineering.)

The Spirit of the Games: Olympic Village

On a slightly larger scale, Vancouver's Southeast False Creek Olympic Village, built to house athletes in the 2010 Winter Olympics, was a very ambitious neighborhood-scale project that is just now finally coming into its own. Just as the Olympics are meant to inspire and show us the best possible human performance, so too did Vancouver have lofty aspirations for the Olympic Village. For Goran Ostojic, who was the project manager for all the systems in the village, "It was an excellent project, but it was too early by ten years for public acceptance of sustainable features."

Tearing down industrial warehouses, developing an old industrial site and bringing urban renewal that would long outlast the games, the city saw the

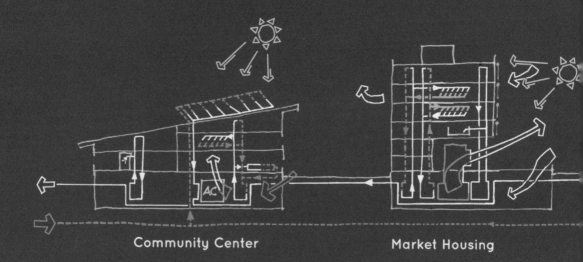

OLYMPIC VILLAGE BUILDINGS

Community Center   Market Housing

project as an opportunity to strive for greatness in community design when all the world's eyes were on it.

The village takes up nine city blocks, consisting of 1100 residential units. "It was two-million square feet done in two years, in a market collapse, during one of the toughest times in North America," says Ostojic.

Because of the project's ambition and the market conditions combined with a difficult timeline, there were issues with financing, deadlines, and politics. "And it was all on the front page," says Ostojic. Not all of the press was good and the politics and spotlight from the Olympics added an odd dynamic to the project. "Probably the most intriguing part for me was being involved but not being able to speak," says Ostojic. "I learned about the huge impact of the media. It can swing from extremely bad or extremely good, and we were caught in the middle."

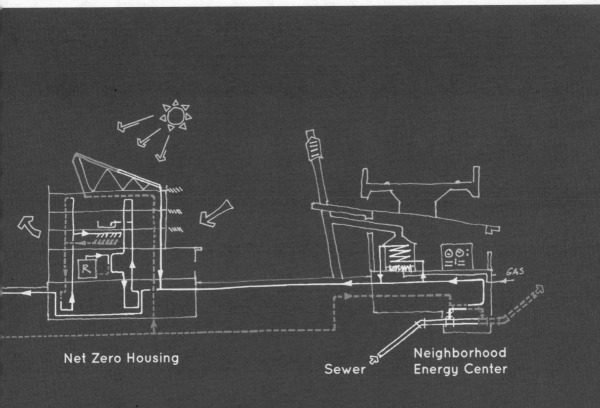

Net Zero Housing

Sewer

Neighborhood Energy Center

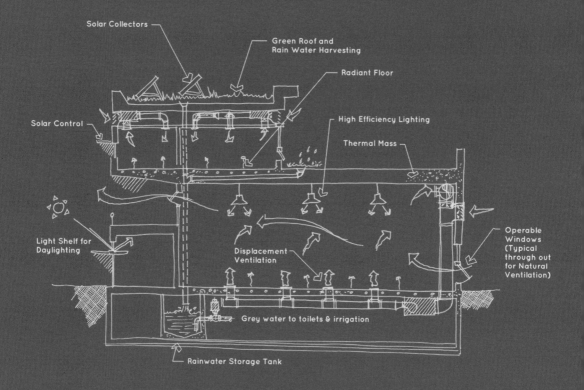

Solar Collectors

Green Roof and
Rain Water Harvesting

Radiant Floor

Solar Control

High Efficiency Lighting

Thermal Mass

Light Shelf for
Daylighting

Displacement
Ventilation

Operable
Windows
(Typical
through out
for Natural
Ventilation)

Grey water to toilets & irrigation

Rainwater Storage Tank

OLYMPIC VILLAGE - CREEKSIDE REC CENTER

But from an engineering perspective, it was an amazing project. "It doesn't get the exposure that it deserves from a design point of view because of all the politics and financial issues that have happened with it," says Ostojic. "We worked with the different architects on glazing and optimizing the buildings. The energy use is 40 percent better than a typical building," he adds. A different architect worked on each of the nine parcels, but Intégral worked on systems for the entire district.

Walking through the village, Ostojic points to the shades on southern balconies that automatically track the sun and self-adjust accordingly. (Intégral ran energy modeling to calculate the solar gain on the south.) The shades draw and rise automatically. A deliberate lack of shading on the north improves natural daylighting where solar heat gain is not an issue. Radiant heating and cooling also increase comfort for residents. Visible pools of water in the community public spaces celebrate rainwater harvesting. The collected rainwater feeds toilets and fountains throughout the village and irrigates green roofs. Ostojic points out that stairwells in the buildings are open and, therefore, not heated or cooled, saving energy. Narrow streets give the community a pedestrian-oriented and European feel. (Visitors not lucky enough to walk through the village with Ostojic can take an audio green building tour by calling a number posted on signs throughout the neighborhood.)

On the edge of the village, Ostojic points out the community building, where activities such as daycare, physical fitness and games, group activities and gatherings all take place. The community building is outfitted with absorption chillers, solar cooling, and blackwater treatment.

Some things you won't see walking through the village include the district energy system, heat rejection through parking structures and a significant percentage of heating and hot water coming from the sewer.

All buildings in the village are LEED certified, qualifying the community for LEED for Neighborhood Development, USGBC's community-scale certification standard.

Like a true village, the community is complete with stores, cafes, taverns, a pharmacy, a grocery store and a liquor store that are all part of the development plan. This complex has drawn other new development in the area, which can take advantage of these amenities.

As the neighborhood settles into Vancouver and the surrounding areas develop, people may forget the politics and the press in time. Vancouver will take lessons learned from the Olympic Village experiment as it attempts to fulfill its goal of being the world's greenest city by 2020. Walking around Olympic Village now, 95 percent occupied three years after completion, it feels likes it's on its way.

A Sustainable D.C.: Walter Reed

The private sector and market demand may drive sustainability, but as Vancouver's Olympic Village, Title 24 in California, and Mayor Richard Daley in Chicago have proven, political will is a great motivator.

"This is a story of the mayor of D.C. going on record as saying he's going to make D.C. a model of sustainability," says Tom Simpson as he begins to describe the redevelopment of the Walter Reed Army Base, a district-scale development, larger than the Olympic Village and even more ambitious in terms of sustainability goals. Rather than using LEED as a benchmark, the city is using energy goals. Simpson says this is a more concrete way of achieving a sustainable development.

The former Army base now being redeveloped was a medical center and was closed down under the government's Base Realignment and Closure (BRAC). The base is sixty-five acres in a fast growing area of single-family homes. (A portion of the site will be State Department embassies.) Three and a half million square feet of existing and new building space will be redeveloped as a mixed use community. Many of the existing buildings, including the original army hospital, are historically significant and will be conserved as such, even with new systems.

Sustainability goals set for the site are phased. For waste, Washington, D.C. wants 50 percent of landfill waste reduced by 2020 and by efficient resource use, stringent recycling and implementing curbside composting, the city intends to hit zero waste by 2030. For energy and carbon, D.C.'s goal is net zero energy by 2030, carbon neutral by 2040 and carbon positive by 2050. For water, the city is shooting for zero site storm runoff and 100 percent greywater reuse by 2020, with blackwater treatment by 2030.

The redevelopment has not yet begun and Intégral has so far been involved on the reuse planning team that has made recommendations for ways to reach

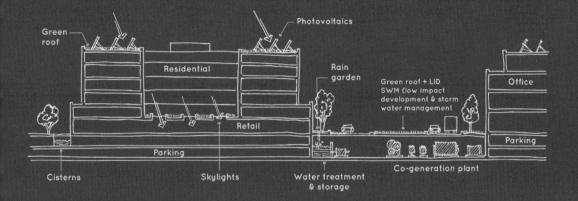

WALTER REED REDEVELOPMENT

these goals. At this time, D.C. is searching for a master developer so the exact development plans are not yet solidified.

"It was an interesting process because we were meeting with all the regulatory agencies in the District, departments of water, energy, utilities, etcetera and meeting with attorneys on regulatory changes," says Simpson. Some existing local regulations do not allow blackwater or greywater systems, and Intégral recommended what will need to change in order for the project to meet its goals.

Butler did an analysis of all the planned buildings and existing buildings and set the energy use index for the building types. The planning team set goals and standards for maximum energy use for every building type. "We proposed using the existing central heating and cooling plant as a temporary system for existing occupied buildings until the new CCHP and distribution could be put in place," say Simpson. "We're working on a strategy to use gas-fired turbines with energy recovery to create cooling and heating from the central plant to cool and heat the buildings combined with PV on the roofs," says Simpson. To achieve net zero carbon and net zero energy, the team wants to find a source of biomethane gas. There is a wastewater treatment plant nearby, the biggest one on the East Coast, where they are already recovering methane. "If it's not from there, somewhere in the future we're sure this biomethane gas is going to be fed into the natural gas distribution system, similar to the way you can buy green power off the electrical grid, and this system will be ready for that," explains Simpson.

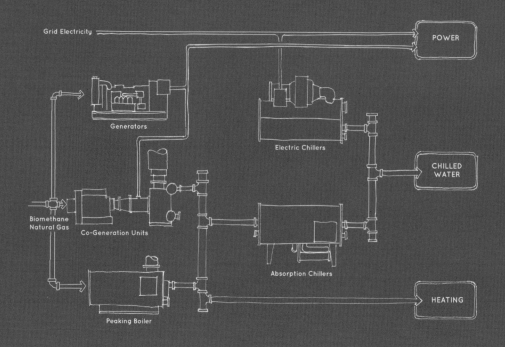

POWER

Generators

Electric Chillers

CHILLED
WATER

Biomethane
Natural Gas

Co-Generation Units

Absorption Chillers

HEATING

Peaking Boiler

WALTER REED TRI-GENERATION

Thinking on a district scale like this may bring greater benefits, but also poses greater challenges. "It's a lot different than saying we want this building sitting on its little island to achieve certain things," says Simpson.

"We are creating power and cooling and heating for 2600 residents plus workers and retail. We are literally creating a small city. But the buildings no longer need chillers and boilers. The efficiencies of the systems go up. The ability to transfer energy back and forth goes up because residential energy needs peak at night while office buildings peak during the day," explains Simpson.

In addition to analyzing building energy indexes and goals in the D.C. area, Butler is working on a carbon-neutral district system in Edmonton, Alberta that will rely on excess sewage sludge from the landfill and timber recycling that provides waste wood. Biomass is a common fuel for district systems in Canada. While it may be net zero water and waste, the Alberta project cannot qualify for the energy portion of the Living Building Challenge neighborhood-scale certification administered by the Living Future Institute because it relies on biomass. While less harmful than fossil fuel, Living Future maintains that biomass poses serious problems.

District Systems and Bridge Fuels

"What if the world wholesale switched to biomass?" McLennan asks. "You can imagine the burden placed upon our productive landscapes to produce this biomass, not to mention there is still air pollution generated. You also have to truck this fuel around. So it may be better than the oil paradigm, certainly better than getting oil from the Middle East, but biomass is not perfect. There's going to be pressure on land that shouldn't be used for converting biomass to fuel."

"The other side of the cycle is the whole nutrient cycle on the planet and soil depletion," he explains. "We have a global crisis emerging around peak phosphate and nutrients in soil and soil depletion and feeding people, not to mention how much we should use arable land to feed people versus growing fuel to burn. When you extract biomass and burn it you are, in essence, starving the land of its nutrients."

No one is suggesting that we really switch wholesale to the bridge fuels, at least in the case of biomass. In the case of natural gas, many people are so excited about it as a fuel that it is being promoted beyond a bridge fuel and fracking is like the new global warming in terms of denial; many people with a vested interest in exploiting natural gas think it is a solution unto itself and just do not believe drilling causes serious harm.

"Let's not get stuck on the bridge; let's go to the solution," McLennan urges. "The solution is solar and wind," he adds. "The difference between solar and biomass now in terms of first costs are not that great. There's plenty of sun to power our civilization many times over, so that's why I'm not that excited by biomass."

"It's like the patch if you're a smoker," he says. "It's slightly weaning you off a really bad habit but it's still not good to put nicotine into your body."

Our addiction is so fierce and entrenched that we a need the patch. But McLennan brings up an important caution. Can the bridge inhibit our quest for a better solution? We cannot allow our interest in the bridge fuels to delay us too long from moving to a better energy paradigm.

Leave No Trace:
Summit Bechtel Reserve

West Virginia is a place that understands how an energy paradigm can shift. "So much of West Virginia was coal mining. That industry tends to move around where the coal seams are. They depleted most of it in this area and now they've turned to wood and logging," explains Simpson, who is managing the engineering for Glen Jean, West Virginia's Summit Bechtel Reserve.

The Reserve is on old brownfield, once a coal strip mining site. "It's a beautiful property adjacent to the New River Gorge, which has some of the best white water rafting in the world," says Simpson. A 1200-foot high bridge over the river is also a popular spot for base-jumping.

"The Reserve is going to breathe new life into that whole region," he says. Like the army base, the Reserve development is like a small city, but for quite a different purpose and populace.

The story of the project began when the Boy Scouts hired Trinity Works developers from Fort Worth, Texas to develop the 11,000 acres of the West Virginia land as one of the Scouts' national base camps. Every fourth summer, 50,000 youth from all over the United States descend in troops on the area for the Scout's two-week national jamboree. The site will also be used for summer camps and high adventure training and education.

"The Boy Scouts leadership decided they wanted to change the face and image of scouting and make it more current by incorporating more adventure such as rock climbing, extreme biking, zip lines, etcetera," Simpson explains. The leadership also declared at the outset that they wanted a net zero community and Trinity brought together five of the deepest green architects in the country and selected Intégral to work with all five architects on the engineering.

The team planned a high-adventure theme park that will serve Scouts' interests in activities like bike and trail riding and rock climbing. Intégral worked on the buildings in the village core and the infrastructure. The village core consists of thirty-two buildings, constituting a little under half a million square feet on sixty-five acres next to a man-made lake.

Each of the architecture firms is designing five to seven buildings, clustered according to a theme or purpose. For example, there is an architect for the 5-7 food buildings, an architect for theater and media technology buildings, and an architect for the two Living Building Challenge buildings.

To meet net zero for the whole community the team decided to go with a geoexchange system. Originally, the team had the idea to run water through coils in the bottom of an old mine shaft for the geoexchange system. Incorporating the mineshaft would link back to the history of the site and the story of West Virginia. But the closest mineshaft was a mile and a half away, so they opted for another novel approach. They tied coil loops to the bed of the lake and they will use the lake water as a resource for the heating and cooling.

The waste treatment installation runs through a PV field, a convenient location for it on the site. "The rainwater capture system is kind of cool," says Simpson. The rainwater is channeled to the lake and the system pumps from the lake. The lake water is then treated and used in restrooms for toilet flushing. The lake is a big natural cistern, so they were able to eliminate all other man-made cisterns, which saved a lot of money. (Simpson has since proposed this idea on other projects as well.)

"We're using a wide variety of systems for heating and cooling, including radiant systems," says Simpson. "We are trying not to design complex systems for buildings that are only going to be used three (summer) months out of the year."

But what was really interesting about this project was the process. The developer and former Eagle Scout Isaac Manning and his facilitator Allison Schapker, Director of Design and Sustainability for Trinity Works, thought there might be something useful about sequestering a design team in a few cabins during a winter snowstorm in the wilderness for ten days, and Simpson agrees, there was.

167

"The integrated design process started from day one, and that was all driven by the developer," he says.

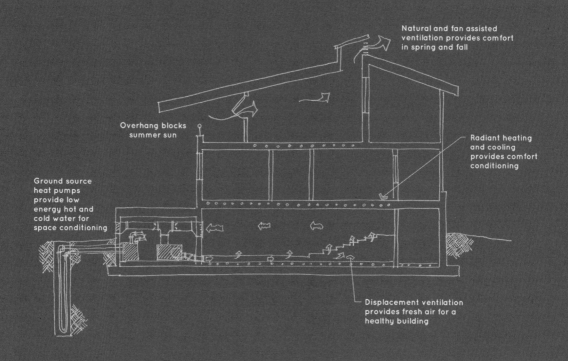

Natural and fan assisted
ventilation provides comfort
in spring and fall

Overhang blocks
summer sun

Radiant heating
and cooling
provides comfort
conditioning

Ground source
heat pumps
provide low
energy hot and
cold water for
space conditioning

Displacement ventilation
provides fresh air for a
healthy building

SUMMIT BECHTEL RESERVE

"We showed up for a workshop in January 2011 in the mountains of West
Virginia. The day we got there it snowed twelve inches. And it was really cold,"
Simpson recalls.

The architects, engineers, developer and Scout leadership all stayed in a white
water rafting facility "with really nice cabins," according to Simpson, for the
duration of the ten days. And during those ten days, they figured the energy use
for thirty-two buildings, plus had hundreds of conversations about strategies for
heating and cooling. It was sort of like a ten-day charrette that was incredibly
effective for building consensus.

"We went through every single building with the Boy Scouts, the architects,
and the developer and questioned, does this building need to be heated? Does
it need to be cooled? Is it used three, seven, nine months a year?" They talked

about the use and comfort goals of every one of the thirty-two buildings, every one unique in some way.

In addition to net zero energy and waste, they had enough rainwater capture that the camp could have been net zero water. The Scouts had already signed agreements for purchasing sewer and water to help the local economic infrastructure. The project possibly could have qualified for the full Living Communities certification from the Living Future Institute if not for their decision to purchase water.

There are, however, examples of Living Buildings such as the Sustainability Treehouse, on the site for the Scouts to learn about. A steel frame that is built into the tree canopy, "the Sustainability Treehouse is 3000-square-feet of the most unusual spaces you've ever seen in your life," says Simpson.

"It was sort of ten days of hell in many ways because the days were just horribly long," Simpson recalls. Following the intensive fourteen to sixteen hour work sessions, the conversations inevitably continued because the developer strategically teamed up cabin mates. Simpson was with two of the principals of BNIM. This was an interesting move by the developer. Through the cabin arrangements, the developer assured the teams were starting to develop relationships.

While the days were long, the process was incredibly effective. The connection between the team members nurtured through the intensive integrated design process inevitably served the goals of connecting the systems and the buildings in a community-scale development, and it shortened the schedule and saved resources.

"The amount of stuff that we created in ten days for thirty-two unique buildings was pretty much off the charts," Simpson says. This approach sped up the process for schematics, which were finalized by the end of February, the month following the meetings. This would normally be a three-month process, says Simpson, still enthusiastic and amazed by the consensus building and the results of those ten days. "This is definitely a once-in-a-lifetime project."

A Living Community:
SFU Campus

While the Bechtel Reserve comes close to qualifying for the Living Building
Challenge Living Neighborhoods designation, the first community to officially
strive for the designation is underway in British Columbia on the Simon Fraser
University campus. The community came out of the earlier work on the
SFU Childcare Centre building we discussed in the Accelerate chapter.

"The SFU Childcare has been wildly successful, economically and
environmentally and people just love it and so they were encouraged to
go much deeper," says McLennan. In the next stage of development, SFU
Community Trust planned 1000 units of housing along with accompanying retail
and parking and associated amenities. "Originally they were going to locate
it in an area with a lot of mature trees and steep slopes. We began working
with them on infilling parking lots and using already disturbed sites and we're
developing a living community for them," says McLennan.

"Living Neighborhoods provides an overarching vision for truly resilient
communities," explains McLennan, who created the concept. "It's on the same

SFU Living
Neighborhood

scale as LEED ND, but we handle it differently because we are trying to produce regenerative communities." So, energy, waste and water are all net zero or better. Living Neighborhoods also consider food a critical part of sustainable and resilient communities and designation as a Living Neighborhood or Living Community requires food production. The less dense the development, the greater the food production required.

"The Living Building Challenge has a Scale Jumping overlay to allow multiple buildings or projects to operate in a cooperative status," according to the Living Future Institute.

The SFU campus is designed around solar principles so it can be a net zero community, meaning 100 percent of the energy the community uses over a year will be produced using on-site renewables. It is also being designed to handle all wastewater and storm water on-site through constructed wetlands, according to McLennan.

"On the planning side we are trying to learn some lessons from the facility itself," he says. Drawing again on the Reggio Emilia educational approach the Childcare

SFU Living Neighborhood

"WHEN YOU START TO BRING INFRASTRUCTURE INTO A RELATABLE, KNOWABLE SCALE, IT OPENS UP OPPORTUNITIES TO TEACH AND INFORM AND RECONNECT PEOPLE TO THE SYSTEMS THAT SUPPORT US AND THAT'S REALLY EXCITING."

relies on, the planning team is asking, "How do we actually create a community that is good for children and how should that fit into community design? What would it mean to create a community that is friendly and conducive to the well-being of children?" Applying this philosophy to the community scale brings social performance in as a sustainability factor on the project. "When you start to bring infrastructure into a relatable, knowable scale, it opens up opportunities to teach and inform and reconnect people to the systems that support us and that's really exciting," McLennan says.

"There's this fit between this scale jumping and decentralized neighborhood-scale infrastructure for energy, water, materials and a philosophy of trying to create wonderful places for people where they care about and understand how their community works and where they understand what's healthy and what's not healthy," he says.

"We're doing net zero energy, and net zero water projects that handle infrastructure issues at a very small scale, but we are also encouraging people to think larger when it's appropriate to do so. We are finding that a sweet spot is often reached at a neighborhood or several block size where the economics of the project also hit a sweet spot as well as that for energy and water," says McLennan.

These communities make sense if our goal is simply to reduce energy use and carbon emissions. And when we face a power outage like Hydes experienced in Ottawa, an earthquake as we expect along the West Coast, or floods and other disruptions resulting from climate change then we must go further. If we are building small communities around district systems and reaching for zero waste, capturing and treating water on-site, generating energy on-site, our communities' hedge against failure of these systems is vastly increased because there is more diversity and resilience built into the system. They truly are sweet spots.

Resilience and sustainability are as inseparable as energy and carbon. All the intelligent, practical, and life sustaining reasons we want to build net zero energy and water and regenerative buildings are reasons to build net zero and regenerative communities. As McLennan explains, it's even more fundamental than that. Indeed, it's our essence. "Regardless of the scale you work at, you need to be regenerative, because nature and life are regenerative."

About the Author: Molly Miller

Molly Miller is Intégral Group's official "Storyteller". She writes about zero energy buildings, Living Buildings, and deep green design and engineering in numerous mediums. Molly comes to Intégral Group from Rocky Mountain Institute, where she was a writer for the Institute's built environment practice. She began writing about sustainable design at *Mother Earth News*, where she was the magazine's senior editor. She helped launch *Natural Home* magazine and served as its executive editor, and has been a staff writer and editor at the National Renewable Energy Laboratory and the U.S. Green Building Council's Colorado Chapter. She has a master's degree in journalism from Columbia College, Chicago.

Credits

Contributors

Great buildings succeed because of teamwork. Many individuals, from Intégral Group, and from other firms, played significant roles on the projects in this book. It is impossible to acknowledge all of them here; however, we are indebted to them for their contributions. This is a partial list of Intégral staff members who shared stories and provided information about their work featured in this publication. Please see Intégral's website for complete biographies.

KEVIN HYDES	Founder and Chief Executive Officer
JASON MCLENNAN	Chief Innovation Officer
PETER RUMSEY	Chief Technology Officer
CONRAD SCHARTAU	Chief Operating Officer
JOHN ANDARY	Principal
MARIA BRIGGS BERTA	Director of Human Resources
TYLER BRADSHAW	Principal
NEIL BULGER	Project Engineer
JIM BURNS	Director of Marketing
TREVOR BUTLER	Principal
ANDY CHONG	Senior Mechanical Designer
SUSAN ECKER	Associate Principal
GERRY FAUBERT	Managing Principal
J MICHAEL GODAWA	Principal
JAMES GOODALL	Principal
STUART HOOD	Managing Principal
DAVID KANEDA	Managing Principal
DOUG KERR	Managing Principal
SK LAI	Managing Principal
LISA FAY MATTHIESSEN	Principal
JOHN MCDONALD	Principal
GEOFF MCDONELL	Associate Principal
BUNGANE MEHLOMAKULU	Principal
VLADIMIR MIKLER	Principal
GORAN OSTOJIC	Managing Principal
HEATHER PEREZ	Business Development Manager
CHRIS PICHE	Principal
SALIL RANADIVE	Principal
TOM SIMPSON	Managing Principal
ERIC SOLADAY	Principal
JEAN-SEBASTIEN TESSIER	Associate Principal
KIM TRABER	Principal
JOHN WEALE	Associate Principal